**Find out the Truth Behind the #1 Show
that Shocked America!**

Hair-pulling, nail-breaking cat-fights and all-in-the-family slugfests have propelled *The Jerry Springer Show* to the top of the ratings. It is the #1 talk show in America, but anyone who has seen the show knows people don't tune in for the "talk."

How did a former mayor and respected political commentator transform himself into television's Sultan of Sleaze? How does he view the show and his role in it? A starry-eyed liberal idealist in his youth, does he really think providing a forum for people to physically attack each other is an exercise in defending every American's right to "free speech?"

Find out who the man is at the center of this hurricane of flying fists. He's not what you'd expect . . .

JERRY SPRINGER

Jerry Springer

Aileen Joyce

Zebra Books
Kensington Publishing Corp.
http://www.zebrabooks.com

ZEBRA BOOKS are published by

Kensington Publishing Corp.
850 Third Avenue
New York, NY 10022

Zebra and the Z logo Reg. U.S. Pat. & TM Off.

First Printing: July, 1998
10 9 8 7 6 5 4 3 2 1

Printed in the United States of America

TABLE OF CONTENTS

Preface

It's a cold and blustery winter morning in Chicago. Despite the below freezing weather, a handful of fans have been lined up outside the NBC Tower huddled together for more than three hours waiting to gain entrance to *The Jerry Springer Show,* the hottest daytime talk show currently on the air. By the time the first of the day's two shows begins taping, an audience of 150 of the faithful and curious have filled the show's second floor studio.

Meanwhile, behind the scenes, Springer is having a meeting with his production staff to learn the topic of the first show of the day. The title is typical Springer fodder: "You Can't Have My Man!"

As the nattily attired, Armani-clad Springer paces the producer's office, his ever-present baseball bat in hand, he is quickly filled in on what the next hour will bring:

"An ex-girlfriend is not only trying to steal back her man, she is seven months pregnant with his baby. She calls him, she writes him—"

"Even though she is pregnant, he doesn't want her?" Springer interrupts.

"Yes," replies the producer.

Without so much as a moment's hesitation, Springer suddenly turns into a baseball coach urging his team on to victory. "Okay," he says, "let's make this the greatest show we've ever done!" Less than three minutes have passed since he entered the office. Not much preparation for an hour-long program, but then Springer makes full use of the show's off-camera teleprompter. He walks out of the meeting and heads for the stage, where he will briefly warm up the audience. Five minutes later he's backstage. After taking two swigs from a plastic container of bottled water, Springer again heads back to the stage for the taping. This time, with cameras rolling and the applause sign blinking, he is greeted by a standing ovation and chants of "Jerreee! Jerreee! JERREEE!"

"She says her boyfriend's ex-girlfriend is not only trying to steal him back, but is seven months pregnant with his baby," Springer reads from the teleprompter attached above the camera. "Let's welcome ROSALIND!"

Rosalind is barely settled in one of the stage's seemingly indestructible chairs when she launches into the usual Springer show diatribe about the woman who "can't have" her man. "Mona sleeps with everyone. She says she's pregnant, but I don't believe it," she quickly tells the spellbound audience. "She calls us all the time, she writes letters . . ."

Springer allows Rosalind to set the verbal stage. Then, with an admonishment to her that Mona *"is* seven months pregnant, so be conscious of that," he announces, "I'm going to bring her out now! Here is . . . MONA!"

Wham! Bam! Slam! Faster than a speeding garbage truck, the two women are on the floor, wrestling, cursing, and tugging at each other's hair. The audience oohs, aahs, and jeers as two of the show's seven bodyguards—all of whom are off duty Chicago cops—jump on stage and attempt to pull the women apart. Not to worry. It's just another typical workday on *The Jerry*

Springer Show set, where an average of four physical scuffles erupt each week.

And where is the show's host during these outbursts? Safely in the midst of the audience, with the show's security staff placed between him and the warring factions on stage, that's where.

Introduction

Shannon wants to make up with her ex-boyfriend, but she has a problem: Calvin works for an escort service, and unless he gives it up she'll never go back to him. What she doesn't know, however, is that Calvin is an escort not for women, but for men. When he reveals that he is bisexual, she starts to cry—and the audience giggles. Moments later Shannon gets even worse news when Calvin introduces her to Anthony, who turns out to be his gay lover. Anthony and Shannon shout at each other, and over the bleeps at one point he can be heard calling her "a gold digging bitch."

Suddenly Calvin's mother appears in the middle of the melee. Strutting up to Anthony, she tells him to "Shut up!" As the pressure rises, the crowd begins to buzz . . . suddenly Calvin's mother and Anthony start shoving each other, and the stage erupts into a tangle of bleeping, indistinguishable curses.

The Jerry Springer Show

A onetime attorney and civil rights activist, as well as a politician and Emmy Award winning TV news anchorman, the mild-appearing Jerry Springer seems an unlikely candidate for the role of ringmaster of the increasingly bizarre circus bearing his name. With his curly, graying blond hair, round glasses, and slightly nasal voice, Springer has a style less empathic than Phil Donahue's and less excitable than Geraldo Rivera's.

He's the intelligent, slightly smarmy observer of the antics around him, not a participant. This may be the peak of his career, but that doesn't mean he will ever be as rich as Winfrey. Major advertisers like Procter & Gamble and Sears shun his show, which can only charge about a third of what Oprah does.

But there he stands, day after day, a slightly bemused observer, calm and affable, a quiet voice of reason largely unheard in the midst of this daily melee of (bleeped) obscenities, hair pulling, gut punching, finger jabbing and inarticulate ravings known as *The Jerry Springer Show.* "I understand the circus that it is," Springer says of the hurly-burly mob scene that often overtakes his show. "People say to me that it's like the Christians and the lions. But some would argue, 'Where are the Christians?' "

Indeed, Springer's guests are the kinds of people you meet only in your worst nightmares—people attempting to resolve their problems by screaming abuse at one another and then resorting to violence. These are the kinds of people who apparently make great television guests, because in the last year *The Jerry Springer Show* has become the hottest, the most controversial, TV show to hit the airways in decades.

Two years after his competitors have either been canceled or abandoned their guests-from-the-gutter format, Springer has turned trash into cash with his show's neverending parade of teenage call girls, strippers, pregnant adulterers, incestuous family members, goose-stepping racists, topless caterers, feuding relatives, freaks, and social misfits. No subject is too indecent, no individual too pathetic, for an appearance on his show.

And it's paid off. In each of the last two years Springer has doubled the number of voyeuristic viewers who watched his show the year before. He even crept up on Oprah Winfrey, The Diva of Daytime Talk, in the last big ratings week of 1997, beating her in Atlanta, Cleveland, and New Orleans, the three cities where the two shows run against each other. He frequently tromps Rosie O'Donnell, The Queen of Nice, in Philadelphia and Baltimore, where they air at the same time. Jay Leno and David Letterman have frequently become ratings road kill in Los Angeles, where they go joke to joke, head to head, with the syndicated Springer show.

Difficult though it may be to believe, if America has become a tabloid nation, then the meek and mild Jerry Springer, with his bespectacled air of a college professor, has become its newly crowned king, thanks to such titillating daily fare as, "My Teen Worships Satan," "I Cut Off My Manhood" and "Honey, I'm Really a Guy."

The Romans had their bloody spectacles. The Greeks had their tragedies. American television has *The Jerry Springer Show*, an orgy of violence and voyeurism that has been likened to "human cockfighting." On the Springer show boyfriends reveal they're girls, and girlfriends turn out to be boys. Wives disclose to their shocked husbands that they're hookers, that they've been sleeping with their best friends, or that they're not the real biological fathers of their sons and daughters. Husbands reveal to their wives that they have other wives, or that they secretly wear their wives' panties. And, in all cases, the TV camera is so tight on their faces that you can almost see through their eyes to the backs of their heads.

Nor are the medically afflicted protected from the insensitivity which is projected daily through guest "ambushes" on the show. Like all the other human wreckage paraded across the Springer stage, they are also trivialized and turned into objects of derision. Take the show "Looking for Love With Tourette Syndrome," as an example. Springer popped the big question to his lovelorn guest: "Lauren, has it always been barking?"

Yet, despite having been dubbed "This Year's Poster Boy for the Decline of Western Civilization" by *TV Guide* and having his show deemed "cultural rot" by several U.S. Senators, Jerry Springer remains unrepentant and unapologetic for the show and its ever-changing daily menagerie of dysfunctional guests.

"Ours is a crazy, silly, outrageous show," he repeatedly explains. "It's escapist entertainment; there's no educational value whatsoever. So how is this ruining civilization? It's chewing gum."

Perhaps his critics are right. Perhaps Jerry Springer *is* taking the low road to high ratings. The fact is that whatever the road he's traveling the journey is leading him straight to the bank . . . and he's laughing at every stop along the way.

THE EARLY YEARS

"I've never stopped being the son of a vendor. You look at the people who voted for me and the people who watch the show. It's the same people. And it's not the hoity-toitys. They are honest, real people. They don't put on airs. They don't necessarily speak the King's English. And they're not wealthy or powerful. They're just people."

Jerry Springer

CHAPTER ONE

Growing Up Poor

"My parents had a real plan
to Americanize me,
and I loved every bit of it."

Jerry Springer

Perhaps it has something to do with being a first generation American. Or perhaps its origins lie in being the only son of the only members of a German-Jewish family to survive The Holocaust. But there are two distinct Jerry Springers. One is a quiet modest man, an earnest, passionate defender of the common folk, an intense philosopher, politician, and historian. The other is a fast talking, quick-witted, guitar strumming entertainer who oozes boyish charm and humor and loves the spotlight. They are opposites living side-by-side in an intriguing bundle of contradictions.

Ask anyone who's ever spent any time with either of the Jerry Springers and they'll tell you he's a warm and gracious, likable guy as prone to quoting Franklin D. Roosevelt as he is to breaking into Elvis impersonations at the drop of a hat. At the same time, if they're honest, they'll admit they don't feel as though they really know him. And that's because, despite all of his rhetorical candor and openness, all of the wearing his heart on his shirtsleeve, Jerry Springer is—and always has been—a very private person by careful design. He's an outsider who lives very much inside himself—a spectator traveling in disguise as a participant, even on his own television show.

Friends have said Jerry enjoys being an outsider, and sees his show as entertainment for people who aren't among society's "elite." Jerry readily identifies with average Americans, and he loves to cast himself as bravely battling the exclusive upper-class.

Gerald Springer was born in England on February 13, 1944, the youngest of two children born to Richard and Margot Springer, Jewish refugees who had fled Berlin in 1939 to escape Adolph Hitler's goose-stepping Gestapo. Other family members were not so fortunate. Jerry's grandparents and several uncles are believed to have perished in Nazi concentration camps during The Holocaust.

So, like the children of many World War II survivors, Jerry grew up without an extended family. And, although he was too young to remember the last years of the war—the nightly air raids, the sirens, the explosions and fires, the bright lights piercing the sky over wartorn London—he was always aware of the guilt and pain his parents felt over the loss of their relatives.

"That's been a major influence on my life," he has said. "Nothing else is even close to that. It was something that was always there, a part of my parents' life that shaped all of us. Six million people were destroyed simply because they were Jewish. If that isn't a fundamental lesson of life, nothing is."

Life in London was difficult for the Springers. Not only did they have to struggle with the language, but they had to fight to survive financially. They had escaped from Germany with their lives and a few clothes, but very little else. The family lived with a distant cousin in Hampstead Garden, a tranquil, leafy suburb not far from Hampstead Heath, London's historic park where Henry VIII and his entourage once hunted deer and fox. Jerry's father was a street vendor who made and sold stuffed toy animals. Margot Springer worked as a store clerk. It was a frugal existence because the Springers had a plan, a dream: they wanted to emigrate to the safety of America, the land of hope and opportunity.

Like the millions of other immigrants who have landed on these shores over the last 300 years in search of freedom, the Springers were in search of a better life for themselves and especially for their two young children—Jerry and his older sister, Evelyn. So they saved every pence, every British pound, they could, and finally scraped together enough money to buy four one-way third class tickets to New York on the Queen Mary in 1949.

Arriving in New York harbor, the family stood at the rail of Britain's famous luxury liner and, like the millions of immigrants before them, watched as the Statue of Liberty welcomed them to their new home as they sailed toward the last hurdle of their voyage: Ellis Island. Established in 1892 as the immigrant depot for processing the greatest tide of incoming humanity in the nation's history, Ellis Island is a symbol of America's immigrant heritage. In its sixty year history more than twelve million people fleeing poverty, religious persecution, or political unrest have landed on the island. Today their descendants account for almost forty percent of the country's population.

In 1954, the year the Springer family became naturalized American citizens, the U.S. government closed Ellis Island which, today, is a museum. But when Jerry's family arrived there the island was still the nation's major port of arrival. First and second class passengers were processed on board the ship, but third, or steerage, class passengers were ferried to the island, where they underwent medical and legal examinations in the main building before passing through Ellis's famous gates of freedom.

According to Jerry's official press biography "He can still recall the sense of awe and anticipation he felt as he first saw the Statue of Liberty and passed through the gates of freedom on Ellis Island. In America, they could live without persecution. Jerry's dedication to upholding the freedoms guaranteed by the Constitution is a hallmark in his life. For his family had seen firsthand what happens when these freedoms are denied."

With help from a New York Jewish Refugee foundation, the Springers settled in Kew Gardens, a predominantly Jewish neighborhood in Queens where Margot Springer's sister lived. The dream had become a reality. Along with hundreds of their neighbors, most of whom were also displaced Jewish refugees, the Springers were safely ensconced in America, but they were still faced with financial difficulties. For the second time in a decade they were beginning life anew, starting over from scratch.

One of Margot Springer's favorite stories about her son harkened back to the days when the family had just moved to Queens. Jerry was about six years old, she told people, when she overheard him ask his sister, Evelyn, why she was home from school on a weekday. When Evelyn explained that it was Washington's Birthday, she heard Jerry say, "Oh, are we invited to his party?"

Once in America, Richard Springer continued working as a street vendor, hawking his homemade stuffed animals, and Margot went to work as a bank clerk. "My dad made stuffed animals and sold them on the street, on beaches, on the boardwalks, and a lot of times he'd take me along," Jerry recently recalled, adding that he always worked alongside his father in the summers, selling stuffed tigers and bears on the boardwalk in New Jersey. "It was the quintessential American dream," he says. "An immigrant family working to the point of exhaustion so that my sister, Evelyn, and I could have this great life."

As Jerry remembers, it *was* a great life, filled with a lot of love, a lot of fun, a lot of adventures. "My parents had a real plan to Americanize me, and I loved every bit of it." He laughs. "We were immigrants coming to the greatest country in the world, a place where freedom was everything." A first generation American, Jerry wholeheartedly embraced life as a child in this country. It is the same fervor with which he continues to embrace America as an adult.

"My family just always seemed liberal," Jerry would later explain. "My parents were Stevenson Democrats. Whatever heroes we had, even in the music world—Pete Seeger, Joan Baez—always seemed to be in the avant garde, caught up in that whole civil rights milieu."

Like any typical American youth, Jerry joined the Boy Scouts and seriously worked on earning his merit badges. He played on the local Little League baseball team. He drank egg creams at the corner drugstore soda fountain, where he argued the merits of his favorite baseball team, the New York Yankees, and the batting record of his childhood idol, the great Yankee's center fielder, Mickey Mantle. He learned to play the guitar and went off to camp for several weeks during his summer vacations. Despite Jerry's idyllic recollections of his childhood, Margot Springer admitted, "We were very strict with him. It was always work before play. I guess it's the German in us."

In 1954, when they could finally afford it, the Springers bought a television set. It was a large set with a small black and white screen, and it suffered from poor reception, but the family sat around it watching the top shows of that era. "When I was a kid I watched, you know, the cowboys—Hopalong Cassidy, Roy Rogers, Gene Autrey, The Lone Ranger. Then as I got older I loved *The Dick Van Dyke Show* and *My Little Margie*. I liked sitcoms, I guess, when I was a kid." He also remembers watching the 1956 political conventions the way some people recall watching The Beatles make their American television debut on *The Ed Sullivan Show.* "With our background," he explains, "politics wasn't just a hobby. Politics had wiped out our family!"

Life was simple and pleasant in the post-war years of Jerry's childhood. And life in Queens was idyllic, especially in the close-knit ethnic neighborhood where Jerry lived. There, everyone knew their neighbors, people greeted each other on the street as they passed, parents didn't worry about their children playing unsupervised, and they certainly didn't worry about sending their children off to school or the butcher shop. Having suffered through the wholesale slaughter of millions during Hitler's rampage, the world and its citizens wanted nothing more than to live in peace. It was the Eisenhower years, a time of peace and prosperity. It was a time when The American Dream was working and saving toward a house in the suburbs, a car in the garage, and a savings account. The violence of the sixties, the sexual revolution of the seventies, and the corporate greed of the eighties were nowhere to be found.

Jerry was a happy child who loved school and loved learning, even though he was a precocious classroom clown throughout his school years. "Oh, maybe I had a couple of bad days," he would admit years later, "but I was totally loved and I loved everything I was doing. I lived a 'Brady Bunch' kind of life."

Years later, after Jerry had become a Cincinnati councilman, his mother confessed she'd always known Jerry was going to do well in the world. "I always knew Jerry was going to be important one day because he was very well liked by his teachers. When he was fourteen, a teacher wrote on his paper, 'We expect great things of Jerry.' "

Despite the love and good times they shared as a family, however, there was always an underlying sense of grief and loss which popped up in strange, unexpected ways—such as when Jerry's parents avoided seeing "The Sound of Music" because it would be too painful. Their experiences became Jerry's experiences. They permeated his childhood and forever shaped his character, instilling in him a philosophy that years later would make it possible for him to become the merry ringmaster of the sleaziest circus in television history: *The Jerry Springer Show.*

CHAPTER TWO

Goodbye Queens, Hello New Orleans

"The lesson of The Holocaust is that you never, ever, judge someone based on what they are. You only judge them on what they do."

Jerry Springer

Although money was tight, Richard and Margot Springer were determined that Jerry would receive a college education. "I grew up in a home where I knew I was either gonna be a doctor or a lawyer. Having lost everything during The Holocaust, education meant the world to my parents," he explains. "They said, 'The one thing they can't ever take away from you is what's in your mind. Be smart.'"

So in the fall of 1961, the year he graduated from high school, Jerry set out on the first leg of a journey that would take him through all the peaks and valleys life has to offer. He enrolled at Tulane University in New Orleans, a town far removed from Queens logistically and philosophically. Not surprisingly, given his background, he enrolled as a political science major.

"I was seventeen at the time and fairly sheltered," he reminisces. "It was a family decision that I should go out of town to college. My high school was so huge—5,200 students—that they could only process the applications for five colleges for every student. So I chose one in every part of the country—Tulane, UCLA, Wisconsin, Cornell, and one in New York. I got accepted to all of them, and I just said, 'New Orleans, what an exciting place to go!'

"Today," he continues, "seventeen-year-olds are much more worldly than back then. So, you know, I was book smart, not worldly. I remember having my eyes wide open, immediately learning about civil rights and thinking, Wow! New Orleans! It was just this massive assault on my senses. This was my first experience with cultural diversity. I mean, really being close to people who had completely different life experiences. I had grown up with people from the same background. So this was really an eye-opening experience for me."

Once again Jerry adapted effortlessly to his new surroundings. "I loved college," he says. "I was not one of those students who couldn't wait until school ended. I enjoyed class. I enjoyed the academics of it." He also enjoyed fraternity life—as a member and at one point chancellor of the school's Tau Epsilon Phi fraternity. He loved rooting for Tulane's sports teams, drinking with guys, and making late night forays into the city's Bourbon Street area which was filled with music, mayhem, and strange denizens of the night, as it is now. He loved playing his guitar and singing.

What Jerry *didn't* enjoy was the racism he encountered in the south. It was his first experience with bigotry, and he was appalled. Remembering the stories he had heard about the Nazi's persecution of the Jews and their second-class status in the years leading up to the extermination camps, Jerry was filled with anger. This was not the America of his dreams. This was not The Promised Land reflected by the Statue of Liberty or the American Constitution.

Determined to fight the racial prejudice he had discovered was so pervasive in the south, Jerry became a civil rights activist while attending Tulane. Later he would become an ardent foe of the Vietnam War and a dedicated supporter of liberal causes, large and small. It is a philosophical and moral stance he retains today, a posture that underscores his actions personally and professionally and allows him to calmly face those with whom he is deeply opposed on his show. "The lesson of The Holocaust," he explains, "is that you never, ever judge someone based on what they *are*. You only judge them based on what they *do.*"

After receiving his degree in political science from Tulane in 1965, Jerry enrolled as a law student at Northwestern University in the Chicago suburb of Evanston. While at Northwestern—a former classmate recalled, "I think he was in the upper ten percent of his class." Springer sang with a folk music group called Springer's Stringers. Later he sang with a partner, a young lady named Linda, under the clever billing of "Linda and Gerry."

In the spring of 1968, Jerry Springer seemed destined for a high-level government job in Washington. But then one of his history professors introduced him to U.S. Senator Robert F. Kennedy, and Kennedy quickly became his idol. (Years later, during *his* early political campaigns, people would liken Jerry to the Kennedys, noting the same clipped phrases and the length of his hair, which seemed to grow progressively longer as the years passed.) Thus, when Robert Kennedy made his late entry into the 1968 presidential race, Jerry took time off from school to travel to seven Midwestern states, trying to woo college students away from Eugene McCarthy and back into the Kennedy camp. He had worked tirelessly in Indiana as one of twelve young people specifically chosen to work on Kennedy's campaign. It's hardly surprising to discover that Kennedy's assassination in June, 1968, sent Springer spiraling into a state of depression. It was, he would later admit, "the worst time of my life."

It was The Sixties, a turbulent time in American politics, a decade of ringing out the morality and sexual mores of the past and ringing in the new. FREEDOM was the byword of the era, whether you were referring to sex, speech, drugs, or marches through the south. Reports of student demonstrations, anti-war marches, police violence, and talk of revolution filled the nightly newscasts.

Then, in two bloody, horrific clashes, it ended, not with a whimper but with a bang. Three students were killed by National Guardsmen during a peaceful demonstration on the Kent State University campus; and the 1968 Democratic Convention turned into a nationally televised blood letting—thanks to Mayor Richard Daley of Chicago and his overly zealous police force, who were turned loose on unarmed but equally zealous protestors. Jerry was in the city's Grant Park, along with thousands of other Vietnam War protesters, watching in horror as the police force brutally attacked everyone in their path, from Vietnam War protestors to innocent bystanders. "It was a strange turning point in my life," he later recalled. "I had just graduated from law school, and so I had the bar to think about in terms of not getting arrested. They were being very careful then about who they were accepting into the profession of law. So there was one part of me that was this anti-war protestor and anti-establishment; and the other part of me that said, 'Wait a second, you can't blow your whole career here!' "

It was a defining moment in American history and an unforgettable experience that forever changed and re-molded scores of sixties college students. Jerry Springer, liberal to the core of his being, was among them. "I really feel like a child of the sixties because all those incredible, unimaginable things really affected me," Jerry would later concede. "I got involved in some civil rights and anti-war marches. And the Kennedy assassinations. Martin Luther King's killing. The Chicago convention. It was impossible to be on a college campus and be oblivious to that."

Like many young adults during the sixties, Jerry got bitten by the political bug. He was angry and thoroughly disillusioned with the misuses of power he had so graphically experienced—and he had decided to do everything he could to change the political system in whatever way he could. "My goal at the time," he would later recall, "was to get the United States out of Vietnam. So I was very active in the civil rights movement and in the anti-war movement. I went into politics to try to get that happening. And I had a very, very fulfilling political life; but I never thought politics would be a career. I think once you make politics a career you sell out because you have to win the next election in order to eat."

Although Jerry had returned to Northwestern and earned his law degree he was uncertain about what he wanted to do, and wound up back home with his family in Queens, where he worked at a series of odd jobs. He was floundering and he knew it, so when he received a call from the Cincinnati law firm of Frost & Jacobs offering him a job in 1969, he jumped at it.

"I was just sitting around in New York. I had to do something to get my life moving again."

CHAPTER THREE

The Big Dream

"If I ever get run out of politics,"
Jerry wisecracked, "I think I can
always get a job as a bingo caller."

Jerry Springer

Jerry had spent the summer of 1967 in Cincinnati working as a summer clerk for Frost & Jacobs, a prestigious law firm, but he had never considered actually living there. "I enjoyed the summer, but I can't say I had any concrete plans to return to Cincinnati," Jerry later admitted. Fate, however, had other plans. Impressed by Jerry's political acumen as a campaign organizer and his ties to the late Robert Kennedy, the law firm people had tracked him down in New York and offered him a full-time position. Thus, in early 1969 Jerry Springer had become an Ohio resident.

Jerry's contact with Kennedy, however, had played a major role in the evolution of his political ideology, and he was far more interested in politics than the practice of law at that point. So Jerry remained with the firm less than a year, having chosen instead to run for Congress, a daring move for someone who had resided in Cincinnati for only six months. Moreover, Jerry was a young, liberal Democrat, as well as Jewish, in a staid, conservative, German Catholic town—and running for election in a district where Republicans outnumbered Democrats 2-1.

Despite these odds, however, the moment he was

within reach of fulfilling the state's minimum residency requirement, Jerry announced his candidacy for the Democratic nomination for the U.S. Congress in November, 1969. At the time of the announcement Jerry was living in a small bachelor pad at the Clifton Colony Apartments and still had to fulfill a four-month Army Reserve training stint at Fort Knox before starting his campaign for the May, 1970, primary.

"I announced for Congress on a Tuesday. On Wednesday morning I received a notice to report to active duty. By Friday I was on active duty at Fort Knox," he would later recall with a laugh. "My opponent in the Democratic primary was Vernon Bible," he added. "It's tough running against a guy named Bible."

Jerry won the Democratic primary, but ultimately lost his bid to unseat U.S. Rep Donald D. Clancy, a popular Republican and incumbent. But it had been "a surprisingly close race." He had run against the conservative Clancy by taking a strong stand against the war in Vietnam, and he had earned an astonishing forty-six percent of the vote. As a result of this political strength, Jerry was appointed by the Ohio governor to head the Ohio Youth Corps.

Despite the failure of his Democratic campaign for a seat in the U.S. Congress, Jerry remained firmly undaunted in his political aspirations. He was convinced that his lifelong passion for politics was a dream to be turned into a reality. So he resigned from the Youth Corps in June, lowered his political sights, and that same month announced he was going to run for election to the Cincinnati nine-member city council. Throughout the summer and fall of 1970, Jerry devoted all of his energies to campaigning, making the usual rounds of meetings, picnics, church socials, and bingo games. "If I ever get run out of politics," Jerry wisecracked, "I think I can always get a job as a bingo caller."

By then Jerry had become a sought after campaign speaker. He had spoken at a Democratic fund-raising dinner where Indiana Senator Birch Bayh had been the keynote speaker. Although he was criticized for often talking longer than he was supposed to, he was fast acquiring a reputation. "Justifiably so," wrote Charlie Bailey, a political writer for the local *Enquirer*, "he has good timing and can mix humor and dead seriousness without losing a beat."

During his campaign for the city council, Jerry energetically followed the campaign trail. He also sang an occasional song along the way, displaying his previously unknown talents at a benefit dance, singing "Blowing in the Wind" to the accompaniment of the Dee Felice Trio, a local jazz group. No wonder the twenty-eight-year-old bachelor was being touted by fellow Democrats as "the hottest political property to hit Cincinnati in years."

Thus it was no surprise that Jerry won a seat on the city council in 1971. It was the first step forward in what everyone believed, and Jerry hoped, would be a brilliant political career. City councilman today, perhaps the Mayor of Cincinnati—better yet, maybe even the Governor of Ohio—in a couple of years. And then . . . who knows? Life was becoming everything he'd wished and hoped it would be. Life was good. No, it wasn't just good, it was GREAT! God Bless America!

"When Springer, young, Jewish, liberal, immigrant, was asked to explain his overwhelming political success in old conservative WASPish Cincinnati, he shrugged his shoulders and was uncharacteristically at a loss for words," a reporter wrote in the early seventies. "Finally," he said, "I don't know—when you look at it on paper, it really doesn't make sense, does it? I guess all you can say is I've touched a nerve here."

Asked by yet another reporter if he could explain his meteoric political rise, Jerry fell back on his penchant for self-effacing good humor. "Luck, pure luck," he replied with a smile. "Being in the right place at the right time. Being well received."

Ironically, more than twenty-five years later Jerry Springer is still touching nerves, and with pure luck has once again managed to be in the right place at the right time. Only these days it's not called the city council. It's called *The Jerry Springer Show.*

Once installed as a city councilman, Jerry added a lot of zest to the staid community of Cincinnati, even going so far as to hijack a bus from the Fountain Square ceremonies celebration the day the city took over the local bus service. He drove it around the block. On another occasion, posing as a vagrant, he spent a night confined in the Cincinnati Correction Institute, a century-old confinement facility known as The Workhouse, ostensibly to check out the jail conditions.

A month later Jerry appeared for a special guest shot on Bob Braun's television show, the *50-50 Club,* and sang several songs with the Apple Butter Band. He recorded a single, "Save the Union Terminal," a plea to revitalize the Cincinnati train station, as part of a one million dollar fundraiser. He popped up on the Nick Clooney show, crooning that song and "Bobby McGee" into the microphone while accompanying himself on the guitar.

But everything was not fun and games for Jerry.

In fall, 1973, he spoke at a Democratic Party fundraising dinner and gave an emotional account of his parents harrowing experiences in Nazi Europe. He detailed how they had fled to England to escape Hitler's tyranny, and how those family members who had stayed behind had perished in Hitler's concentration camps. He had concluded the speech by telling the audience, "So, if your friends don't understand why you care enough about your government to come to a dinner like this, you tell them to ask my folks." It was a line he would often use in the future, usually to his best advantage, over the next twenty-four years.

In March, 1973, Mr. and Mrs. Joseph G. Velten of Cynthiana, Kentucky, announced the engagement of their daughter, Margaret, a University of Cincinnati student, to Mr. Gerald Norman Springer, vice-mayor of Cincinnati and the only bachelor on the city council. The two had met four years earlier, in August, 1969, when Margaret, a secretary at Procter & Gamble, had asked a fellow employee to find her a date for a Saturday. She was going to a movie with her sister and brother-in-law and didn't want to be a fifth wheel. The friend called Gerald Springer. "It was the best blind date you could ever imagine," she would later recall. "He was totally different from anyone else I had ever dated. He was totally uninhibited. I guess it impressed me because I'm so worried about what other people think. Now I realize that's just Jerry."

"The key thing was when I found out she's a Democrat," Jerry joked shortly after their betrothal had been announced in the local papers. The couple were married June 16, 1973, but didn't leave on their honeymoon until several weeks later when the city council recessed for the summer.

Margaret, whose nickname was Micki, was the perfect wife for Jerry. She was strong, smart, and totally dedicated to her husband and his political aspirations, but she was shy and not at all interested in being in the political spotlight. "I'm quite pleased with all the publicity Jerry gets. He's quite a public person. When someone describes him as a charismatic, electric, personality I have to agree. Yes, most people say you either love him or hate him. I support his self-fulfillment, and I expect Jerry to support mine. In marriage two people can't be happy together unless they are happy independently. I give Jerry my total support to allow him to get himself into situations that are both challenging and rewarding."

Like many women of the sixties, Micki had her own life, her own dreams, her own career plans, and her own opinions. "I totally support the women's movement," she said in a 1977 interview. "I think it is immoral that we are still trying to decide whether women should have equality, the right to make choices, the right to make our own decisions."

She had left her home in Kentucky in 1964, moved to Cincinnati, and had landed a secretarial job at P & G shortly after her high school graduation. In 1971 she'd begun attending classes at UC, and at the time of her marriage she'd been only a year away from receiving her bachelor's degree in elementary education and following her dream of teaching children in grades from kindergarten to sixth grade.

"Secretarial work was all right," she once told a reporter, "but I had sat behind a typewriter for seven years. I wanted to work with people instead of paper and machines." However, Micki had confessed several months after the wedding that she didn't plan to teach all of her life. "We want to have children, of course. There are a lot of things that go into deciding whether to have children. Maybe I'll teach a year or two before we do," she had said.

Jerry and Micki spent the first year of their marriage living in a Western Hills apartment in suburban Cincinnati. "We're still in the midst of decorating it," Micki laughed months later. "We're trying to do it as cheaply as possible," she'd explained, pointing to a dining room table they'd had refinished and the living room drapes she'd sewn. Since they were busy attending social and political events, they relished spending their leisure time watching television, reading, and talking. "I learn a lot from Jerry," Micki told a reporter. "I value his opinion."

In late 1973 she also was looking forward to her Jerry's very bright political future. "I want him to go as far as he can," she said. "It's amazing how happy it makes him to be successful."

And Jerry *was* successful and very, very happy as 1973 turned into 1974. He had been re-elected to the city council for a second term. By then he had won by such a landslide that the council had decided to name him the city's new mayor. The ceremony was to take place on December 1, 1974, in city council chambers, before the lights and the cameras and the flowers. His parents were still alive, and Jerry reported, "I've already been instructed to get a haircut. Some things never change," he joked.

Once he took office, Jerry would have made his mark in American politics by becoming the only person other than Senator Hubert Humphrey (D-Minn), to have served as the mayor of a major American city at the age of thirty. Thus, in the early months of 1974, the name Jerry Springer was all over the local news.

Watchers of local politics gushed over Springer's charisma and irresistible charm. Unlike many staid, overly serious politicians, Jerry came across as intelligent, articulate and dedicated, yet he radiated a sense of fun and enthusiasm that many of his colleagues lacked.

In late March, 1974, the local *Enquirer* even ran a front page story titled "Springer Sometimes Brash, Unorthodox," in which the writer described Jerry as "the young man with the sandy tousled hair and the slightly owlish look when he dons his glasses presents a picture to the public that is somewhat less than the haberdasher's dream. But," the writer had added, "when he speaks on the issues before a crowd he can summon the fire and grand phrasing reminiscent of the Kennedys."

"Maybe so," wrote another reporter, "but his arguments against the war in his ringing Eastern accent grated harshly at times upon Cincinnati ears."

With this kind of notoriety, Jerry was in a jolly mood, joking with reporters about his upcoming installation as mayor. "I've got to get a new suit," he replied when asked about his plans for the future. He also admitted, "It's obviously exciting, but I'm a little nervous, I guess. You know a lot of experienced people have gone before me in that job. People who were kind of like pillars of the community. Highly qualified people. I'm not interested in being like every other mayor, of course. But I do nevertheless recognize the success they had and," he'd concluded, "I'd hate to ruin our winning streak."

Even Micki Springer allowed herself to be profiled as the city's soon to be First Lady, although the reporter later acknowledged she offered "No practiced smiles, no handshaking secrets" during the interview. The twenty-eight-year-old wife was "all business," explaining, "To me, being the mayor's wife just means the husband is a mayor. Until today," Micki had confessed, "I hadn't thought of it as a role." She was not, she confessed, a politician's wife like Pat Nixon or Lady Bird Johnson, and she didn't like public speaking. "I can see myself in a situation where I could speak to small groups," she confided, "but I am petrified of large groups. I do go around to campaign with him, though, and in the summer I went to all the festivals," she conceded. "I've received several invitations to join women's clubs in the city, and I'm flattered," she'd added, "but I don't have time to be an active member, and I think it would be selfish of me to join if I don't."

Apparently sensing his wife's discomfort, Jerry joined the conversation, telling the reporter, "She didn't run for office, I did. She's her own person with her own interests," Jerry had explained. "She doesn't expect anything particularly of me because she's a teacher, so I don't expect anything particularly of her because I'm a councilman. We're just two people in love."

But not everyone was in love with Jerry. Not everyone was under his charismatic spell. In an April 4, 1974, column in *The Cincinnati Enquirer*, political columnist Frank Weikel penned: "Well, last Sunday during the charity telethon on WKRC-TV, newsman Charles Bolland pledged (without my knowledge) that if a thousand dollars was raised during his hour on the program that I'd say something nice about Springer.

"The station raised not a thousand . . . but $2300 during that hour. So since then I've been trying to think of something nice to say about Springer. However, after four days, I give up."

CHAPTER FOUR

The Nightmare

"There was never any run-in with authorities. I was never arrested. In 1971 I slept with a prostitute—actually, I didn't sleep the whole time."

Jerry Springer, 1997

Jerry was on top of the world in March, 1974, but only a month later that world collapsed, sending his political career into an abyss from which it appeared it would most likely never be exhumed. The very fame he had acquired became a nightmare overnight when *The Cincinnati Enquirer* ran a blind gossip item titled Behind The Scenes on April 29, 1974. In the item Frank Weikel, the newspaper's political columnist, wrote:

"A well known Cincinnati political figure is currently the subject of a vice investigation that is under way in both Ohio and Kentucky.

"Word is that in the Kentucky investigation the figure and his attorney have already had 'an interview' with federal investigators and a federal prosecutor.

"In Cincinnati authorities have not talked to him about association with a prostitution operation, but I have learned that several prostitutes have been interviewed and all tell stories that link him to a health club operation."

The item had ended ominously with "LOOK FOR THIS STORY TO BREAK INTO HEADLINES IN THE NEAR FUTURE."

Speculation ran rampant through the City Hall corridors, across local talk radio and over backyard fences as the citizens of Cincinnati tried to figure out just who that "unnamed" politician might be. Names floated up and over Cincinnati like the wisps of smoke emanating from the city's skyline of tall smokestacks. Yet no one came forward—until the following day when Jerry Springer stepped forward and, in a most unconventional manner, announced his resignation by tacking a note to the door of his city council office. The note said:

> "It is with deep personal regret that I am announcing today my resignation from the city council. I understand what I am giving up, an enormous opportunity to share in the leadership of this great city. However, very personal family considerations necessitate this action. My family must and does come before my own political career. Thank you all for all you have given me. I hope that I have offered something positive in return."

With Jerry's installation as mayor already guaranteed to take place, his sudden mysterious resignation left everyone in numb disbelief. The citizenry, the press, even the state's politicians, from the Ohio governor to the Mayor of Cincinnati, were in shock. At the state capital Governor John J. Gilligan called Springer a "brilliant young man." William A. Lavelle, the Democratic Party state chairman, called Springer "one of the brightest in the galaxy of stars we have in the Democratic Party here in Ohio."

"It was a complete shock, a complete surprise to me. I had no prior indication, nor did any other councilman that I know of. It was a blockbuster surprise," confided the outgoing mayor.

Since no one could locate Jerry, the resignation re-

mained clouded in mystery, but apparently not to everyone. By the end of the day the city's political leaders
were tight-lipped about Jerry and would not talk to reporters. By Tuesday evening everyone understood why
Springer had resigned.

"More than any other politician in town," wrote Bill
Furlow, political reporter for the *Enquirer,* on the day
of Springer's resignation, "Springer produced strong
feelings in people. Some disliked his liberal political
philosophy and called him a 'giveaway' politician. Others said his ego and his ambition were destined to cause
him to take an early fall. But many people viewed Springer as a symbol of the 'new politics,' as a public official
who offered the hope of a better day."

On Tuesday afternoon, with Micki watching tearfully
from the sidelines, Jerry held a news conference in a
third floor committee council room at the Cincinnati
City Hall. He appeared tired and red-eyed from a lack
of sleep and nervous, shifting from one foot to the
other during the questioning. The press conference began with Jerry reading a prepared statement:

"When I resigned yesterday, I did so because I
believed then as I believe now that there are some
problems which are better faced as a private citizen.
I am currently confronting such a problem.

"On two occasions I have been a customer of a
'health club' in Northern Kentucky and engaged
in activities which, at least to me, are questionable.

"These actions have weighed heavily on my conscience. Early last week I contacted the FBI and
voluntarily answered all inquiries of what I had
done and of what I had knowledge. I am continuing
to co-operate in that investigation in any way that
I can.

"I believe the interest of the public is best served

by my resignation until such time as the air has been cleared."

Jerry then proceeded to field questions from the horde of reporters as the TV cameras rolled in the crowded room right off the city council chambers. The barrage of questions went on for almost an hour.

Q. Why didn't you explain things yesterday when you resigned? Why did you avoid the press for twenty-four hours?

A. Nobody . . . there's no way you can possibly understand what it's like unless you've been through it.

Q. Why did you go to the FBI at this time?

A. Because it was—that club was under investigation. It was across the river, and it's been in the newspapers and oh, television, and I heard of that investigation and I immediately . . .

Q. Were you involved in that investigation?

A. Oh, no. No way. I said I was a customer over there. These rumors—there have been—as much as people have been very nice to me, there have been some incredible, incredible stories about me involved in some kind of ring . . . hearings before grand juries in Lexington . . . just ridiculous stories that are totally untrue. My involvement has been as a customer. I find that unsatisfactory enough.

Q. These unquestionable activities—were they prostitution or gambling?

A. Well, it was not gambling.

Q. Were the visits paid for by check?

A. Yes.

Q. Isn't that unusual?

A. Yes. Very unusual.

Q. What were the amounts of the checks?

A. I don't remember . . . I don't recall.

Yes, he finally admitted, he had been involved with

two prostitutes who operated within a "health club" located in the President Motor Inn in nearby Fort Wright and on both occasions—in December and January—he had paid for services rendered by writing a personal check. Yes, he had voluntarily met with the FBI the week before, and had answered all of their inquiries as to what he had done and what he knew. No, he had not been arrested. No, he was not facing any criminal charges.

Jerry then said he had made the decision to resign after discussing the situation with Micki, his bride of only nine months, his family, and her family. "The public has a right to expect a very high standard of its officials," he said, "and I feel I have violated that standard." He then said, "It's a question of how much embarrassment you can accept for yourself and your family."

The press conference ended with Springer saying, "I wish to express my deepest gratitude to those who have stood by me through this ordeal. My wife, my family, and so many friends, those both in public life and private citizens, have given me strength when I needed it most."

Micki, it was noted, wore the same dress she had worn when, just five months before, she had been at city hall to watch her husband sworn in for his second term on the council. "Politics and the council has been Jerry's life, and to give that up would destroy him," she told a reporter. "It's his whole life. He loves it, and he's worked so hard for five years that I can't stand to think of him throwing it all away. What Jerry did was wrong," she added, "but it's nothing to throw your life away for."

Micki then admitted that she was trying to persuade Jerry to stay on the council. "I've never been very political, but I know what Jerry needs to stay alive. I just love him, and I can't bear to see him broken like this," she said. "It means a lot to me that people realize that whatever Jerry admitted has nothing to do with our relationship and our life together. I have been trying to convince him not to resign since this whole thing began," she added. "He had so many plans, so many hopes for this city. I would do anything to see that he gets to fulfill them."

Micki Springer's appearance at the press conference, as well as her subsequent interview, was an amazing testimony of her love for Jerry. Until then she had successfully managed to avoid the public eye.

As Jerry fielded questions at the press conference in downtown Cincinnati, the interstate vice trial had already begun in the U.S. District Court in Covington, Ky. Only three days later Jerry would take the stand and, under oath, admit that he had patronized the Leisure Health Club on two different occasions, and that he had twice paid by personal check for acts of prostitution. He identified the two checks, which he had turned over to the FBI, and he also identified a Ms. Knight and Norma Jean Hall as his sex partners.

On the following day, May 3, 1974, Jerry changed his mind about resigning from the city council. He was sorry he had resigned as councilman so quickly. "I began to think I'd over-reacted," he would later explain. After meeting with the council members and discovering they were supportive, Jerry called a quick press conference, his second in a week, to announce his decision to continue as a councilman. "I cannot possibly condone what I did, and I'll pay for this the rest of my life," he told those convened, "but based on the council's support I've decided the best thing to do is to return to my seat. I have told you the whole truth, the entire truth, of my involvement. I am prepared to take the consequences of what I have done wrong. It is a highly embarrassing situation that has weighed heavily on my conscience. But the initial public response has been that I should not throw away my public responsibility because of it."

Jerry had then pointed to Micki, who was standing by his side, and told the crowd that she had been "the most influential person" in persuading him to change his mind. He had impetuously resigned the previous Monday, he had explained, because "it seemed the only thing to do since I first realized the import of what I had done."

Only later would the public learn that on the Friday prior to the blind item on the front page of *The Cincinnati Enquirer,* Jerry had gathered his family, aides, and friends together at his home. Then, pacing back and forth in front of a curtained window, treading a path between his easy chair and a couch crammed with people, he had come clean about his involvement with the prostitutes.

As the listeners sat in somber silence, Micki had quietly sobbed in the background. Then the phone had rung. "I hear you are resigning," a reporter had announced. It was then that his path became clear. During the weekend Jerry and Micki had huddled with family and aides and drafted the detailed letter of resignation that was to be released early Monday morning. By that time the Springers had intended to be on their way out of the city. But that letter was never released. Instead, because of the item in the *Enquirer,* the resignation note was tacked to the door of Springer's city council office.

But that was then. A week had passed. The worst was over and Jerry, it was noted, was back to being his old assured self. He had faced the worst time of his life. He had told the truth and survived the aftermath. "They can't hurt me anymore," Jerry had confided to friends and family. "I want to stay in Cincinnati. I want to remain on the council."

For several days it appeared as though Jerry might be able to ride out the crisis and remain in office. As it turned out, however, it wasn't to be. The following week letters and telephone calls protesting his return began flooding City Hall. Having come out of their shock, citizens and various politicians had clearly decided it would be best not to condone Jerry's behavior by allowing him to remain in the council. "Maybe, in retrospect, I should have stuck to the original resignation and saved myself the last eight days," Jerry confided sadly to colleagues.

By May 8, it was clear that Jerry Springer was not going to remain a council member. Seven of the eight members voted to remove him. "If they don't want me, they don't want me," Jerry told Micki. "I still have some sense of self-respect and I won't be put in a position of begging."

With the vote in, Jerry was convinced his political career was forever over. "I would hope that you view me as someone who stood up and fought for what I believed in, but also as a human being—one clearly not without sin, but one who had the courage to stand up and tell the truth about his mistakes," he told the council.

"I have not given that much thought to what I am going to do," he told the press. "Right now I think I ought to be concerned about picking up the shattered pieces of my life. The only thing I have now," he concluded," is my wife, and the fact that I have told the truth."

Everything Jerry had so carefully built up in the five years he had lived in Cincinnati had come crumbling down. His image and his reputation were, at the very least, tarnished; more importantly, his long-cherished dream of a political future had been destroyed. Or had it?

Today Jerry laughs about the scandal, explaining "There was never any run-in with the authorities. I was never arrested. In 1971, I slept with a prostitute—actually, I didn't sleep the whole time. Okay, I was with a prostitute in 1974. I publicly admitted to that and there was an uproar back then. So I said 'I resign.' And that was it. I owned up about the prostitute because I thought one day it might be exposed and I could be blackmailed. But it wasn't like I owned up to a murder. It was just half an hour with a girl."

But at the time it had certainly been no laughing matter. "They were beginning to write my obituary," Jerry would later concede, "and I was beginning to believe it. I did feel more dead than alive. Words aren't sufficient to describe how terrible that period was."

CHAPTER FIVE

Just Call Him Mr. Mayor

"I guess part of maturing is to have control of your life and not just be swept away by events. I was almost just observing my life rather than living it."

Jerry Springer

A person with less character and *chutzpah* than Jerry Springer would most likely have quietly moved out of town, leaving the gossip behind and praying that it would soon be forgotten. But Jerry didn't leave town. Instead he joined a small, local law firm in August and kept a low profile for the remainder of 1974.

Throughout the ensuing months, however, his name still continued to crop up in the local newspaper, such as in an October item by Frank Weikel which noted "there appears to be a real effort to revive former Cincinnati City Councilman Jerry Springer as a political candidate. Since resigning from his council seat Springer has continued to attend political functions, and according to Democrat sources his reception has been good."

In late December, Jerry was the subject of a front page *Cincinnati Enquirer* interview in which, once again, he pleaded *mea culpa* for the wrong he believed he had done the city, himself, and his family. "I cry a lot on the inside," he admitted. "It was a horrendous personal situation. And I must have been scarred by it. I must have been. I'm not sure I can articulate it yet, but it did some damage to me as a person. Whether or not the wounds have sufficiently healed in my own person to face all that again, that's what's difficult. And it's a decision I'm going to one day sit down and make."

He was obviously testing the political waters, still unsure about what he was going to do with the rest of his life, telling the interviewer he was still filled with a passion for politics.

"I'm convinced that in order for me to survive as a human being of any particular worth, I've got to do something with my life which is more than making money," he explained. "I've been raised to believe that political participation, government participation, issue-oriented participation, is the noblest thing that you can do with your life. There has to be some justification to why I'm alive, and that's it for me. I'm not necessarily sure that means you have to run for political office," he'd added, "but you do have to be involved."

After admitting that "the most inexcusable, terrible thing is that I could have hurt Micki," whom he described as "an incredible person, a much stronger person than I am." Jerry had confessed that the hardest part of having his life opened up to the public had been "the incredible vulnerability." "I tend to be a fairly aloof person outside of my public image," he had explained. "I guess they say it a lot about comedians, which is a bad analogy in my case, but people who are always on the public stage, or performing, have it as a defense mechanism for some very basic insecurities. And so, all of a sudden, there was no façade. There was no joke that was going to carry me through the moment. All of a sudden, there I was, as vulnerable as a human being can be, in front of the world—in front of at least *my* world. Everybody who's ever known me now knows about it.

"It doesn't just go away," he added. "I could not go to sleep. And when I woke up in the morning if I did sleep for an hour or so, it was there. It wasn't like, 'Oh, gee, what a bad dream I had.' It was there. It was real. It was on the front pages of the newspaper, on television. It was standing on a street corner waiting for the light to change, hearing a couple of people behind me either snickering or making some wisecrack, or staring, the incredible stares that to this day don't let up. I'm sitting in a restaurant, and it's a real event, you know. 'That's him.' "

Jerry had ended the interview by telling the writer, "In the back of my mind there's always the feeling that I have a particular talent in the area of government, and it just feels like somehow it has to be put to use. There are very few things in this world I know how to do, but that was one thing I was good at. I was good as a public servant, and it's a shame to put that talent to waste.

"On a professional level," he'd concluded, "I feel somewhat unfulfilled because I'm not doing what I could be doing. I keep thinking I could be doing something that is really significant to an awful lot of people and to the community. And right now, I'm on the outside."

But Jerry wasn't on "the outside" for long. The following year, 1975, when the Democrats refused to put him on their ticket, he ran as an independent for a seat on the city council. And once again he won.

"The whole thing," he would later confide, referring to his political death and subsequent resurrection, "has been an incredible maturation process. You can't be the same person going in as you are coming out of it. I know my own limits now. I know what emotional strains I can handle, what political strains I can handle. It made me a little more confident as a person. And," he added, "I've learned that you don't live alone in the world."

Two years later, in his 1977 bid for re-election, Jerry

stunned even himself by emerging as the top vote-getter in that year's 24-candidate race for the city council, a race in which he outstripped his closest rival by nearly 10,000 votes. "I was absolutely shocked at how well I ran," the slender, boyish-looking Springer conceded. "It was a weird sensation for me as the results came in and my lead steadily widened. I was pretty confident I would be re-elected," he added, "but I had no illusions about leading the field." Jerry was thirty-three years old and still the city's political Wonder Boy, but now he'd also earned a new nickname—The Comeback Kid. "I have never sat down and mapped out my political career," Jerry told reporters. "Right now, I'm most interested in becoming mayor—I'm not hiding that fact. After that," he'd added with a shrug, "I really don't know about my future."

But Jerry's longtime friend and campaign manager, Mike Ford, understood the landslide vote for his candidate, and thought he knew what was in Springer's future. Ford believed Jerry could reach great heights as a politician. "He had a personal connection with the voters that frankly baffled a lot of us," Ford would recall years later. "He had a work ethic that was incomparable and a gift for relating to every person he met. He'd say 'When people wonder why I spend so much time walking the streets and knocking on doors, the answer is, ask my parents.' "

"Springer," penned a local reporter, "the former anti-Vietnam War activist, the self-styled liberal Democrat, the former butt of half the dirty jokes told in Cincinnati, thinks most voters of whatever political persuasion judge him basically on the kind of job he is doing in city government."

"I know it's self-serving to say anything about my job," Jerry countered, "but I think the public knows I work hard at it, dealing with constituent problems and providing services. If I can get their streets fixed, they're not going to care whether I'm a liberal or much about what my political views are." He was correct. The citizenry loved him, even if the local politicians were skeptical about his actions.

"He was very committed to politics, and to liberal policies," recalls John Kiesewetter, television critic of *The Cincinnati Enquirer.* "He had a nice, self-effacing sense of humor."

Despite his gigantic win, however, the position of mayor did not come to Jerry without a certain amount of angst. A winning Democrat also wanted the position and held out for it until the last moment. A local reporter, Karen Garloch, was at Jerry's home the night he learned that he would, indeed, be the mayor of Cincinnati. She captured the scene as Jerry spoke on the phone and Micki hurriedly straightened up the living room in anticipation of the media arriving at their home. She was still trying to clean the house when the newsmen began arriving. While Jerry manned the constantly-ringing phone, accepting congratulations, Micki watched the camera crews set up their lights and string their wires. "I don't think this makes me more a politician," Micki told a reporter, explaining she was not really sure what the role of the mayor's wife should be.

"I don't know that I thought he would be coming this close to mayor again," she admitted to another reporter, "but I knew he would be successful. I have confidence in him." Then, as she had during those three, long, often dark years before on the eve of Jerry's sex scandal, she told the press, "I'm just not the kind of person who can speak before large groups. That's just not me."

She spent the rest of the evening pleading with photographers not to take her photograph. "You don't know how I hate this," she said of publicity, adding, "I know you want to interview me, but I can't stand it." Off to the side, Jerry was humming a song, holding a television microphone, speaking to the media and grinning like he'd never grinned before. "Last month," he told a reporter, "the people spoke."

A week after Jerry had officially been sworn in, becoming the youngest mayor in the city's 189 year history, a local editorial stated: "Councilman Springer is all but certain to bring to city hall both a new style and a new substance." The writer was absolutely correct in his assessment of what was about to become Jerry's mayoral "style."

Actually, Jerry's reign as the mayor of Cincinnati was not much different than in his previous years as a city councilman. It was filled with high-spirited fun and games. He was then, as he is now, a man of the people and enormously popular. He would frequently show up unannounced at some of the city's folksy coffeehouses and spend the evening playing his guitar and singing. Once, when the circus was in town, he even wrestled a bear. And when the Beach Boys appeared in concert, Mayor Springer officially greeted them, jumped up on stage, and joined the group for a rousing chorus of "Good Vibrations."

But behind the happy façade, the good times and the ever-present sense of humor, there rested a great sadness for both Jerry and Micki. It had nothing to do with Jerry's political career or their marriage, or the sex scandal of two years before. It had to do with the birth of their daughter, Katherine Suzanne, on July 7, 1976, at Cincinnati's Good Samaritan Hospital. Within hours of the tiny baby's arrival, it had been discovered she'd been born physically challenged and that she was going to need, at the very least, a series of operations.

Jerry was devastated and Micki was distraught to learn

that their daughter, who had been placed in intensive care and had been receiving oxygen since her birth, was facing surgery only the day after she'd been born. The situation was dutifully recorded in the press, which quoted Jerry as saying, "Katherine will be undergoing surgery tomorrow because the nasal passages in her nose are not completely opened. The doctors are going to open the passages, widen them, and then insert tubes to keep them open until they heal." Five weeks later Katherine finally was released from the hospital and, accompanied by a smiling Jerry and Micki, got to go home.

Then, in late September, the couple received more tragic news. Katherine, whom by then they were calling "Katie," had also been born legally blind as well as deaf in one ear. The doctors also believed the child was possibly mentally retarded. "That really knocked the wind out of Jerry," a close friend said at the time. "He was just getting back on his feet when they found out about Katie." Shortly after the devastating news, Jerry announced to the press, "We are obviously crushed," Jerry told the media, "but we are determined to give her the fullest life a child can possibly have. It appears to be a situation that cannot be corrected by surgery, but we're still consulting with specialists. We're hopeful that sometime in Katie's life, something will be developed."

Several months later the doctors revised their diagnosis. "The doctors are amazed," Jerry jubilantly announced. "She's not totally blind, by any means. She sees things. How much, we can't tell for sure. She has some developmental problems, but we're encouraged. It's been like a miracle. At least we have hope now."

Not long after Katie's birth defects had been discovered Jerry told several friends that her afflictions had changed *his* perspective on life. "Her eye problems have helped me to see better what is really important and what isn't," Jerry had explained.

Two years after Katie's birth a reporter visited the Springer home. By then she had just begun walking on her own, much to her parents' delight. "You're really seeing something new," Jerry proudly explained. "She's been furniture walking up to now. When you don't see, you don't explore," he added rather plaintively.

"She's seeing a lot more now than any of us would have guessed," piped up Micki, recalling how two years before she and Jerry had taken their two-month-old daughter to the doctor for what they believed was to be a routine examination. It was on the same day Jerry's parents were coming in from New York to celebrate his mother's seventieth birthday. "I remember I kept asking myself, 'Why doesn't the doctor hurry up so I can get to the airport?'" Jerry said. The reason, the couple soon learned, was that the doctor had discovered the baby was blind. "It wasn't easy to hear someone say, 'Excuse me, your daughter can't see,'" Jerry recalled. "It was good to have the family around at a time like that."

Further tests showed that Katie suffered from *coloboma,* an impairment of the optic nerve that cannot be corrected by surgery. "We all have blind spots in our eyes but hers are much larger," Jerry explained. "The doctors told us she would be able to tell between light and dark, but they didn't know what else. Now she seems to be learning to use what she has. She seems to be able to see things up close."

"We were told that she was blind," Micki injected. "We weren't optimistic. It was a real shock but we were able to handle it. Now that she seems to be able to see; it only makes us feel that much better."

Today Katie is a twenty-two-year-old intelligent, confident college student in Chicago. She and Jerry are extremely close, and she remains, as always, Jerry's top priority and the love of his life. "Katie is what's important in my life," he told an interviewer recently. "Television is only television. It's not real life, but it's a fun way to make a living. I think Katie was the reason I was given these (financial) resources. It was to be able to help this kid."

In July, 1994, Jerry penned a series of essays for *Woman's Day* magazine. The first was a Father's Day column in which he proudly pointed out, as he often had to friends, that Katie was the *only* member of the family who could run for U.S. President because she had the distinction of being the only Springer to be born in this country.

"Katie was born with a whole checklist of problems," he acknowledged, "but she's overcoming them all. Now she's in college, doing fine. It's just a really happy ending."

CHAPTER SIX

Farewell, Politics

"This commercial should be proof that I'm not afraid of the truth," he said in the ad, "even if it hurts."

Jerry Springer

Jerry absolutely loved being the mayor of Cincinnati, even though it was mainly a ceremonial position. He had faced the worst days of his life and had not only survived them, he had flourished. He was still that happy child from Queens exuberantly living "A Brady Bunch" kind of existence, only now he was living it on a much higher level. Rarely a day passed that his name wasn't mentioned in one of the two local newspapers or his face didn't flash across the television screen. Jerry seemed to be everywhere—speaking at luncheons or dinners, shaking hands at fundraisers, political and otherwise, turning up for impromptu singing appearances, guitar in hand.

Jerry even began showing up at local radio stations to read the homespun commentaries he'd written on subjects ranging from local bond and sewer issues to the untimely death of John Lennon. On one occasion during an appearance on WEBN-FM's early morning "Daily Briefing" program, Mayor Springer satirically announced to listeners that he was planning to clear the city streets of everyone, including police, by 9:15 P.M.—"to allow muggers to mug themselves!"

Some things apparently never change. Jerry Springer loved the limelight then. He loves it now.

In February, 1978, Jerry appeared at Bogart's, a Cincinnati nightclub. As a last minute stand-in for an ailing magician, he entertained a crowd of several hundred people for twenty minutes. He had bounded on stage dressed in a casual sport coat and slacks, open-necked shirt, and a sweater. Then, all the while protesting he was not a comedian, he sat on a stool in the middle of the stage, fielded questions, and tossed quips at the crowd, such as telling them he had been born in England but had left when he learned he could not be king. Jerry had wrapped up his appearance by presenting a key to the city to Leo Kottke, the guitarist and singer, who was the star of the show. Then he bounded off stage to a standing ovation.

A month later, Jerry took his act on the road by traveling to Hollywood, where he made his national television debut as a guest on the daytime Dinah Shore show. The invitation to appear had come shortly after Jerry had joked and Dinah had sung during the Greater Cincinnati Chamber of Commerce's annual dinner clambake several weeks before. The chamber of commerce members had been so impressed with the offer that they actually paid Jerry's way to Los Angeles and put him up in a Beverly Hills hotel.

When Jerry returned home several days later he was filled with quips about the trip, telling listeners that when he'd arrived at the CBS talent gate he'd immediately felt out of place. "I was the only one there not in a Mercedes. They thought I was there to help clean the studio," he joked. He also laughingly lamented, "On the way to the airport, no one stopped me to sign me to a movie contract even though I kept sticking my head out the window looking for talent scouts."

Jerry had displayed his sense of humor in front of the TV cameras, too. Appearing on the show during a cooking segment with Dinah and a chef, he'd immedi-

ately confessed, "I don't even know how to fry an egg."
Later, when the proper preparation of Ohio fish was
discussed, Springer said he hoped the fish was not from
a river in his state. "If it is," he quipped on camera, "it
probably died *before* it was caught."

No wonder that in May, 1978, Margot Springer confided to a Cincinnati reporter, "We don't care what step
he takes next, as long as he doesn't go into show business. That's just too tough a field." Back then, of course,
Margot Springer was thinking of jokester Jerry's singing
and guitar playing. There was no way she, or anyone
else, could have envisioned *The Jerry Springer Show,* with
its daily slugfests and its parade of moronic guests and
bizarre freaks. Until the 1990's such a show would have
been unthinkable, a bad dream of *Twilight Zone* proportions.

"Being mayor," Jerry would reminisce after becoming host of the popular *The Jerry Springer Show,* "was the
most fulfilling job I have ever had. This job now is the
most fun. But this has nothing to do with that, other
than being how I make my living. It doesn't have anything to do with who I am."

Despite the enjoyment he'd derived from being Cincinnati's 1970's answer to New York City's 1930's "Gen-
tleman" Jimmy Walker, Jerry was politically ambitious
and was seeking higher levels of political satisfaction.
He'd never hidden that fact from anyone. And one of
his aspirations was to be the Governor of Ohio. He saw
that as a stepping-stone to even greater heights, like the
U.S. Senate. "Sure, I'm ambitious," Jerry once told an
interviewer, "but, gee, I didn't grow up wanting to be
president."

"Those familiar with Springer's all-consuming passion for politics," zinged a political pundit in reply,

"might say that's only because the U.S. Constitution doesn't permit naturalized citizens to become president. And," the local columnist had concluded, "many would agree with the wry observation made recently by Mike Ford, Springer's closest political adviser: 'Jerry will take care of that—once he gets to the senate!' "

So, with the encouragement of his advisors, in 1981 he decided to make a run for the exalted position of governor of Ohio instead of running for re-election to the city council. As it turned out, it was an ill-fated idea. Relinquishing his job as mayor, Jerry plunged wholeheartedly into his campaign to become the Democratic nominee. It was going to be a tough and costly contest against two of the state's most powerful politicos, and Jerry knew he was the decided underdog in the three-way race. But he was not about to toss in the towel or abandon his dream. "I'm tougher than I look," Springer told a reporter. "I'm not just a wide-eyed kid gazing around in amazement. I'm aware of my political possibilities in the future."

He was also aware of the political liability the sex scandal of 1974 would create. Still, he remained undaunted, even going so far as to appear in a TV commercial harking back to the prostitution scandal. "This commercial," he told viewers, "should be proof that I'm not afraid of the truth, even if it hurts."

Jerry believed in the truth. He also believed that the truth could never truly hurt anyone, including someone like himself who had fallen from grace smack in the middle of the public eye. "By this time, I suppose I've heard all the Jerry Springer jokes. So, personally, I know I can face that again," he told an interviewer shortly before launching his campaign. "Politically I don't see it as a big obstacle. The point is," he added, "they can't talk about '74 without talking about what's happened since then—leading the ticket, getting to be mayor. The

more they talk about '74, the more remarkable the
comeback appears."

"Springer is a master at attracting media attention,
which arouses a mixture of admiration, envy, and antagonism among his council colleagues," penned a political reporter in a *Cincinnati Enquirer* editorial. "His
sense of political timing is close to impeccable; whether
the issue is a carbon tetrachloride spill or an inordinately
cold winter. Springer almost always is ahead of colleagues
in gauging public opinion to find the 'right' position.
Springer realizes that he's regarded as a politician who's
only too willing to jump on the soap box on any issue.

"He makes no excuses for that—in fact, it fits perfectly into his conception of a public official's role,"
the editorial continued. "But that attitude, combined
with his considerable ambition to move up the political
ladder—yes, he hopes to someday be governor or U.S.
senator, he'll tell you—is precisely what makes it hard
for many persons to determine the bottom line on Jerry
Springer. Does he speak out on so many issues because
he has deep convictions about all of them or merely
because he wants to grab the political spotlight?

"Most political observers believe it's a little of both."

"If I learned one lesson from the sixties, it's to get
on the *Six O'clock News,*" Jerry countered. "Civil rights
and anti-war activists showed that you could influence
public opinion by getting on the news."

Not by coincidence, then, did television become a
key weapon in Springer's arsenal during his campaign
for the Democratic nomination. He spent $200,000 in
the two weeks prior to the June 8, 1982, primary for a
series of ads outlining his ideas for Ohio, all of which
he wrote himself. They were simple spots, with none of
the cheering throngs of admirers or patriotic music

playing while flags waved in the background. The commercials were just Jerry sitting on a stool, facing the cameras and making a pitch for the people of Ohio to join him in turning the state around.

"I'm the only person running on the Democratic side who has been involved in the running of an urban government," he told viewers. "I've had to live my issues for ten years. I had to vote on taxes and hundreds of other things."

As he had in all of his campaigns, Jerry also took to the stage, guitar in hand, to sing at various fundraisers, including a noon concert on Cincinnati's Fountain Square. Although he was wearing a suit and looked more like a conservative banker, Springer turned back the clock and sang an original song he'd written in the sixties, as well as a couple of country-rock tunes.

"One way to get me to stop singing is to make me governor," he told the audience of mostly pinstriped professionals on their lunch break.

"Springer has one of the broadest political bases I've ever seen," said a longtime politician. "He has the youth vote, the blacks, the blue collar vote, the intellectual liberals, the disadvantaged, the elderly—it's the damnedest coalition I've ever seen."

In mid-April, after the first of three debates between Jerry and his opponents Richard Celeste and Bill Brown, several polls showed Springer moving ahead of Brown, the favorite, and not far behind Celeste. At that point, he later recalled, euphoria had reigned in his camp. "For a while there, we got worried about what we would do if I won."

As the campaign wound down and the primary election drew near, however, Springer had sensed he probably would meet the same fate as independent John Anderson had in the 1980 presidential race, when many

of his early backers decided that a vote for him would
be a "throwaway vote."

"To be honest about it," Jerry said, "I think a lot of
people thought Dick looked more like a governor than
I did. The maturity factor worked against me."

He also said one of the biggest ironies of his campaign was that his internationally publicized television
commercial dealing with the sex scandal had actually
received more exposure on television news programs
than it had as a commercial. He noted that the ad had
only run twice in Cleveland, the state's largest market,
and had never been telecast in Cincinnati. "Yet," he
concluded, "everyone seems to know about it, not just
in Ohio but all over the world."

Jerry spent election night glumly viewing the early
returns on television from a suite at the Imperial House
North hotel, telling friends, "I don't think I can win"
and cursing his luck over the violent thunderstorm that
had struck Cincinnati in the late afternoon, flooding
and closing polling places. "Bill Brown and Dick Celeste must have seeded those clouds," he laughed, referring to his opponents.

Earlier that evening Jerry and Micki had dined with
some of his most generous campaign contributors. After dinner he'd danced an impromptu jitterbug with
his five-year-old daughter, apparently in an attempt to
ward off the blues. "I'm scared stiff," he told a friend.
"I've got two years and two million in contributions in
this campaign, and it looks like it all could go down the
drain."

Later that night he secluded himself with his family
and close friends in a hotel several miles from the hub
of election night excitement in downtown Columbus.
The hotel was chosen, explained Moss Murphy, Jerry's

press secretary, because it was operated by a close friend. "If we win, it doesn't make any difference where we are because the press will find us, anyway. If we lose, it's a good place to hide," Murphy joked.

Any mirth in the Springer camp that night, however, turned out to be short-lived. Although Jerry received high praise as a good campaigner full of fresh ideas, he finished exactly where he had begun in the three-way race: LAST.

The June, 1982, primary marked the end of Jerry Springer's involvement in the political arena because, even though he had forthrightly admitted his entanglement with the two prostitutes eight years before in his campaign advertising, it was widely believed that the issue was a significant factor in his poor showing. And that stain, when it came to politics, was not going to be easily, if ever, eradicated. True or not, Jerry to this day still believes "the public appreciated the honesty."

After losing the campaign, Jerry threw his support behind his former opponent Democrat Richard F. Celeste, who was subsequently elected governor of Ohio. He had decided, at least for the time being, not to return to politics. It was a decision that would change his life forever and lead him down a twisting, often bizarre, road to fame and fortune—not as a politician, but as a television personality.

CHAPTER SEVEN

Hello, TV!

"It isn't tough being an anchor. If you can get over the nervousness, you can learn it in a month and a half. If the red light is on, you talk."

Jerry Springer

After losing his bid for the Democratic nomination for governor, Jerry spent the remainder of the summer of 1982 working as a paid consultant and fundraiser for the Ohio Democratic Party making appearances on behalf of Richard Celeste. He was thirty-eight years old, deeply in debt after losing the nomination, and unsure of just what the future held. The $2500 a month he was earning as a consultant was simply nothing more than a stop gap measure to buy time and bring money into the Springer household while Jerry figured out what he wanted to do next. It really didn't take him too long to decide.

After taking a long hard look at his political future Jerry, ever the practical person, realized that he had few political options. If Celeste won the election, and he appeared to be a shoe-in, it would be four years, maybe even eight, before Jerry could launch another bid for the governor's mansion. And, locally, the only positions of interest to him were congressional seats held by deeply entrenched incumbents. The other option, a cabinet post if Celeste won in November, had been rumored; but Jerry wasn't genuinely interested in being a cabinet member. It just wouldn't have offered him enough visibility, enough freedom. With his personality, showmanship, and style, he knew full well that he would have had a difficult time making the transition from team leader to team player.

So, two months after his defeat in the primary Jerry announced his plans for the future: He was giving up politics for television. He was joining WLWT-TV as the station's nightly news commentator for an annual salary reportedly between $75,000 and $100,000! God Bless America!

"This is what I'm doing for the foreseeable future," Jerry told the press. "Right now, I'm departing elective politics. You ask me if that means forever? Forever is a long time. Ten years ago I wasn't even living in Cincinnati," he added. "Right now, I'm making a decision to go into television. So this is what I'm going to concentrate on.

"I don't need to be a candidate to survive. The issues facing the community are larger than partisan politics. I don't feel I'm leaving the subject matter. I'm just leaving the prospect of being a candidate."

Upon learning of Jerry's decision to join WLWT a local politician laughingly pointed out that Springer was in "a rut for threes. He finished third in the primary race for governor. Now he's with a station that is number three in viewer ratings for its news."

Ironically, Jerry made his television debut on November 2, 1982. It was election night in Ohio and, had he been the news anchor Jerry would have announced that Richard Celeste had been voted into office as Ohio's new governor. But the anchor job was still far in the future. Instead Jerry Springer made his first appearance as a genuine TV personality by delivering a commentary in the 11 P.M. news segment *Nightbeat*. The subject of his first commentary was *himself*, and his hope of becoming "a social commentator" who could offer an interesting and different perspective on news events. The biggest problem with his new job, Jerry confessed on air and off, was finding the discipline to write every day.

"It's really strange to do something new. All my life I've done two things: go to school and be a councilman," Jerry told an interviewer shortly before his debut on the news. "On city council if you had one new idea a month you were leading the pack."

With the same fervor he had exhibited in politics, Jerry launched into building a career on television. He had a contract—"It's a relatively long-term contract for this business," he'd told friends—but he was desperately in need of money to pay off his campaign debts. In fact, only the month before he'd taken to the airways the Internal Revenue Service had filed a tax lien of $21,726.24 in back payroll taxes against his campaign committee—and that represented only a small part of the reported six-figure debt. Although the financial burden rested with the committee, it was still an embarrassment to Jerry, someone who until recently worried a great deal about public opinion and his image as an honest and forthright fellow.

Just as he now writes his "Final Thoughts"—delivered at the conclusion of the Springer show—Jerry sat at his desk and jotted down his thoughts for his WLWT nightly two-and-a-half-minute commentaries on a yellow legal pad. He always wrote after the 5:30 P.M. newscasts because, he explained, "I like to see what the stories are, and see what the phones are going crazy about." The commentaries were an extension of the "Springer Memorandum" he had delivered on WEBN-FM back when he was a councilman. By the time the commentaries had been transformed into "Final Thoughts" on his talk show, Jerry had become a seasoned veteran when it came to condensing his thought on two pages of legal size paper. "When I get two thirds the way down the second page," he once laughed, "I know I have to bring it home." Interestingly, the commentaries were then—as they are now—the one thing in TV land to which Jerry appeared to be totally dedicated. "I honestly don't know if I could do this job if I couldn't do the commentaries," he would tell the press. "Not that it isn't a nice job, it just isn't what I want to do in life. For that I sacrifice what I'm not able to be, at least in the viewer's minds—warm and cuddly and all that. Every night I'm making a lot of people angry.

"Writing commentaries is so intellectually stimulating. In politics," he explained, "after you develop basic issues, you tend to repeat them day after day. With the commentaries, you're forced to create something new every day. There are not many jobs in the world where you have to create something new, every day, from scratch."

As he had in the political arena, Jerry had a meteoric rise in the television business, even though not everyone was impressed with his commentaries. "Don't be deceived," wrote a *Cincinnati Enquirer* columnist a week after Jerry's TV debut. "Jerry Springer, the fast-talking, wisecracking commentator, is really a sheep in wolf's clothing. His furious pace and snarling humor serve mainly to hide the fact that not much is being said.

"A longtime politician with a gift for gab, Springer dresses up his otherwise mushy commentaries with some of the most bizarre one-liners this side of *Saturday Night Live*. When Soviet premier Leonid Brezhnev died, Springer wondered aloud, for instance, whether some of Brezhnev's Kremlin buddies might have held a towel over his head until he suffocated. Sometimes," the reviewer concluded, "these rapid fire jokes are funny, but more often they serve only to hide the lack of any real point of view."

"You gotta love that Jerry Springer fellow," wrote another local columnist. "He stumbled over the same spot in his commentary three times the other night, even looked dead into the camera and admitted he'd 'lost his place.' And yet, he could laugh about it and put viewers at ease by ending with 'If you'd like a copy of my commentary, I'd be interested in seeing it, too!' "

Despite the brickbats being hurled at him by the press, however, a year after joining WLWT-TV Jerry got his first shot at being a news anchor by filling in for the regular anchor on all three of the station's Saturday evening newscasts. "It's just as a substitute. We've given everybody on the news staff the opportunity to get that experience," the station's general manager explained as rumors of Springer's ascension to the anchor job immediately began wailing through the community.

Despite the denials, however, anybody who knew Jerry Springer knew he was on his way to the top once again. And they were right, thanks in large part to a career move by Nick Clooney, then Cincinnati's most popular news anchorman. Had Clooney not left a competing station to move to Los Angeles for what turned out to be a brief stint as the news anchor at KNBC, chances are WLWT would never have promoted Jerry to the position of news anchorman. "You could say they were so low down, what was the risk?" Jerry would later jest.

But Clooney, the father of *ER* heartthrob George and the brother of songstress Rosemary, did leave. Seeing an opportunity to fill the void of popularity and ratings left in his wake, WLWT executives took a big gamble, and in March, 1984, named Jerry co-anchor with Norma Rashid of their 5, 6, and 11 P.M. WLWT newscasts.

"The moves they made were unheard of in the business," Jerry conceded several years later. "They got a partisan politician to do commentary and did not give equal time to the other side. They got a liberal Democrat in a Republican city to give his point of view. And then they also let him anchor!"

Jerry had made no secret that he wanted the anchor job from the moment he'd first negotiated his WLWT contract. Nevertheless, when he finally landed it, he was very nervous. "Here I am, forty years old and I'm doing something new. Of course, I'm nervous," he confessed. Although he had spoken before hundreds of people hundreds of times throughout his political career, Springer found the solitary experience of speaking to a TV camera more difficult and disconcerting than he'd expected. Thus he was noticeably uncomfortable being in front of the camera in those early days.

"At rallies, not everyone pays attention. You can mumble. No one is recording it," he explained, adding, "in life there are no VCRs." Several years later he would admit it had taken him more than to become at ease in front of the unblinking eye. "I reached a point where I'd still sweat when things fell apart," he told an interviewer seven years after he'd joined WLWT, "but now I've come to realize, 'Hey, it's only television!' It isn't tough being an anchor. If you can get over the nervousness, you can learn it in a month and a half. If the red light is on, you talk."

When Springer and Rashid were first teamed up, WLWT-TV news was in solid third place in a three-station town. Together the team built up the ratings until they had parlayed the once third place newscast into first place, a ratings position it held until shortly before

Jerry's 1992 departure to Chicago to host *The Jerry Springer Show*.

In 1985, there was a momentary flurry of rumors that Jerry was headed back into the political arena as Governor Celeste's second in command. But Jerry was no longer interested in politics. He'd fallen in love with television and being in front of the camera. So, to set the record straight for once and for all he sat down and wrote a Letter to the Editor that *The Cincinnati Enquirer* published:

> "There have been two articles in your paper recently speculating on my being Gov. Richard Celeste's choice for lieutenant governor in 1986. They were well-written. They were flattering. They were also wrong!
>
> "They were wrong because Lieutenant Gov. Myrl Shoemaker is the lieutenant governor, and as soon as he gets better, he will run again. He deserves the governor's support, and he'll get it.
>
> "The articles were also wrong because I am not a candidate for lieutenant-governor, or governor, or councilman, or mayor, or congressman, or dog warden. Simply put, I'm not in politics; I'm in television news. I enjoy anchoring on Channel 5. I love being able to write and deliver commentaries every day. I'm working hard at being a journalist; and thankfully people are starting to watch us now in growing numbers.
>
> "I haven't lost my love for a good race. But these days I'm running against Al Schottelkotte and Randy Little. That's competition enough! Now, of course, if there's an opening for king . . . well . . ."
>   Jerry Springer

* * *

With that letter Springer closed the door on his political career and concentrated his energies solely on the various functions of his television news career. As a result, for almost ten years Jerry was Cincinnati's most popular—and definitely the most unorthodox—news anchorman. He had the most exposure of any newscaster in the city because he not only read the news but he also delivered his commentaries at the conclusion of each newscast. In 1987, for instance, Jerry delivered a scathing commentary chiding then presidential candidate Gary Hart for complaining about the media scrutiny of a clandestine liaison between Hart and a woman who was not his wife. After all, he had pointed out, reporters had known about the affairs of Dwight Eisenhower, Franklin D. Roosevelt, John F. Kennedy, even Thomas Jefferson, but didn't report them. "The media believes you should hide these things. And don't flaunt it. And if you flaunt it, we're going to report on it. And that to me is hypocritical," Springer declared.

Having endured his own sex scandal twenty-four years before, it's not surprising that Jerry feels a great deal of sympathy for any public figure enduring scandals of a sexual nature. Perhaps that's why he used the same argument eleven years later to defend President Bill Clinton, whom he firmly believes shouldn't have to face such public scrutiny about his sex life. "It shouldn't be our business," Springer recently said. "Whatever he did in his private life is between him, Hillary, and God. I don't believe any of us would say we shouldn't have had George Washington as our first president because of his affairs with married women," he continued, calling upon his storehouse of political knowledge to bolster his point. "Or that Thomas Jefferson shouldn't have been president because he had children out of wedlock.

Franklin D. Roosevelt got us through World War II. Should people have said, 'It's okay to lose the war, but I want you out of office because you had a mistress?' "

In 1989, to all outward appearances Jerry was still one of Cincinnati's most happy fellows. WLWT was paying him handsomely—enough to purchase an expensive new suburban home and to drive a Jaguar—and he was still enjoying being a part of the TV news community. "Hey, the president of the United States isn't on two-and-a-half minutes a night," he said, laughing. "I'm so happy with what I'm doing, I could do this the rest of my life. I don't know that I will, but I could. This is the best job in the world. And they pay me for it, which is absurd, but I'm glad they do."

But behind the scenes there was trouble in his marriage, and by the end of 1989, he and Micki had quietly separated. It is a marital situation which, almost ten years later, sadly still exists.

For his efforts as both news anchor and commentator Jerry ultimately earned seven local Emmy Awards and was voted Best Anchor by the readers of *Cincinnati Magazine* for five consecutive years during his ten year reign at WLWT-TV. "Jerry was tremendously well-liked," recalls John Kiesewetter, television critic of *The Cincinnati Enquirer,* who has followed Springer's career for more than twenty years. "People listened to him whether they agreed with him or not. After the news he would sit around and take phone calls from people who wanted to discuss what he'd said. Some people think I am absolutely loony when I say this, but his commentaries were oftentimes brilliant."

By 1991, Jerry had traded in his Jaguar and was driving around Cincinnati in a Rolls Royce. Not content to simply remain "a talking head" on the newscasts, by

1991 Jerry had also begun going on location, doing special assignments such as traveling to Ethiopia during an emergency care airlift of supplies and reporting on the country's troubles. In April, 1991, disguised in a scruffy beard, unkempt hair, and aged clothes, Jerry spent six days on the streets of Cincinnati living among the homeless. He dined at soup kitchens, napped in the public library, slept under trestles, and then reported his experiences in a five-part series titled *When The Streets Are Home* on the WLWT news.

As it turned out, the series was to be Jerry's last news special hurrah. Six weeks after the series had run, to the surprise of everyone but Jerry, WLWT-TV announced it would be launching a new daytime television talk show. In addition to his news chores, Jerry would be the host.

THE SHOW

Razberry has been seeing three women at the same time . . . and making false promises to each of them. Razberry's sister is so disgusted by his deceptions that she brought him here to face his girlfriends. Today he'll be forced to choose one or lose all three.

Next . . . Joe is here to confront his best friend for sleeping with his girlfriend, Michelle. But Joe's buddy insists he only did it to prove that Michelle is promiscuous. He also claims to know at least two other guys with whom Michelle has cheated!

"I've Been Unfaithful!"
The Jerry Springer Show
March 13, 1998

CHAPTER EIGHT

A TV Star is Born

"It's like you're in a room with 150 people, and you're working a lounge. If they gave me a band, I could sing!"

Jerry Springer

In early 1991, Jerry was happily delivering the news and his commentaries, as he had for almost a decade, when out of the blue he received an invitation to have lunch with several station executives and Walter E. Bartlett, chairman and chief executive officer of Multimedia Entertainment, Inc.

A corporate conglomerate that owned several television stations, including WLWT-TV, Multimedia was also then producing three of the nation's top daytime talk shows—the Phil Donahue, Sally Jessy Raphael, and Rush Limbaugh programs—and then offering them for syndication. It was a lucrative business and Multimedia wanted to add another talk show to its roster. More importantly, at least to Jerry, they wanted him to host the new program.

Although Bartlett did not voice his concern during the luncheon with Jerry, the behind-the-scenes truth was that Multimedia was looking for a possible replacement for Phil Donahue, who was then approaching sixty and had begun talking about retirement. The company wanted someone articulate, erudite, and nonthreatening like Phil waiting in the wings. In the gregarious Jerry Springer they saw the perfect potential candidate.

"One day they took me to lunch and said, 'We're going to start a new talk show—and you're going to host it!' " Jerry would recall several years later. "They didn't ask me—they assigned me to it. That's how I got it. I didn't audition. I was literally assigned to do the show!"

Jerry's only concern about doing the show was that he did not want to give up his nightly news chores. When he was assured he could continue as anchor and commentator, he enthusiastically accepted the job. In the back of his mind, no doubt, was the recollection of the last local talk show Multimedia had produced in Cincinnati. Hosted by Pat Barry, that show had lasted only seventeen weeks. He had no reason to believe *The Jerry Springer Show* would last any longer than that. And, by keeping his anchor job intact he'd managed to cover his financial bases. If the show was an unexpected success, so much the better, but Jerry wasn't about to gamble his entire television career on it.

Thus in early June, 1991, it was announced that Jerry Springer was going to host a talk show. "Move over Phil, Oprah, Geraldo, and Sally Jessy Raphael," proclaimed John Kiesewetter in his *Cincinnati Enquirer* column. "Make room for Jerry Springer."

"I'm not going to do anything that would jeopardize my bread and butter, doing the news and commentary," Springer told the local media shortly after the announcement. "I'm not suicidal. I'm not going to foul it up by doing something absolutely stupid.

"Would I do things that are probably going to be uncomfortable?" he continued. "Yeah. But," he added, "I do news stories that sometimes I'm not comfortable with. I'm very conscious of the subject matter that some of the other hosts have during sweeps month, and there are some things that I probably would say, 'I just can't do it!' For instance, I will not be dancing with The Chippendales. I can tell you that because I've been promised that I would not have to do that. I would object to that. But," Jerry concluded with a laugh, "remember who you're talking to. I'm the guy who sang with the Beach Boys at Riverfront Stadium!"

With the crew in place by early September, 1991, the show began a round of rehearsals on September sixteenth. Production officially began exactly one week later, when the first ever *Jerry Springer Show* was taped before an audience of 150 people in the gray and rust studio walls of WLWT-TV's fifth floor studio in downtown Cincinnati. Multimedia, it was reported, had spent hundreds of thousands of dollars on the Springer show—from the huge TV studio where it originated to the olive gold suit and red necktie with huge brown magnifying glasses worn by Jerry in his debut.

In its earliest incarnation the Springer show was a far cry from the bizarre and outrageous show it is today. It was an easygoing knockoff of *The Phil Donahue Show,* a talk show in the truest sense where people calmly discussed serious issues of the day—like gun control, the plight of the homeless, runaway kids, AIDS and timely news events, such as the Waco massacre.

Although the show dealt with emotional issues and still offered the usual sensational subject matter, it was a far more thoughtful and provocative program than it would eventually become. There were no violent outbursts from the plethora of guests, who ranged from Oliver North to the Reverend Jesse Jackson. There were no screaming, no inarticulate ranting, no bleeped obscenities, and no lewd exhibitionists parading across the screen naked with only black bars shielding their most private body parts from the home audience. In fact, the debut of *The Jerry Springer Show* on September 30, 1991, was not a particularly auspicious event in the annals of television talk show history. Produced in the TV backwaters of Cincinnati, the show was only telecast in Los Angeles, Dallas, Cleveland, and Mobile, where Multimedia then owned TV stations.

However, Jerry could not have cared less about the number of stations carrying the show. Having entered his third career at age forty-seven, he was thrilled and excited about the show. "How many rushes in a life can a person have?" he asked of no one in particular. "I felt today like the day I was sworn in to be mayor, or the day I did my first commentary or newscast," he said after having taped the first show. "I'm lucky. I'm really lucky.

"I've never done this before," he continued. "You can practice the physical stuff, the running up and down the aisles, and how you hold the mike. But there is no way for you to rehearse for this until you stand out there. It isn't like you've got to memorize your lines. There are no lines. But this is amazing," he gushed to an interviewer. "It's like you're in a room with a hundred and fifty people, and you're working a lounge. If they gave me a band, I could sing!"

When a local newspaper columnist subsequently pointed out that between Jerry's hour talk show, his nightly commentaries, and his anchoring the news, Cincinnati viewers would have twelve-and-a-half hours a week of Jerry Springer, and queried whether that wasn't too much even for loyal Springer supporters, Jerry replied, "To get all of that you'd really have to be glued to the set twenty hours a day. Someone who is going to watch me that much obviously wants to!"

Later asked if he thought he'd appeal to viewers in New York and Los Angeles, Springer shrugged. "I'm either likable or I'm not. I'm not going to worry about that," he said, "I can't control it. Viewers are going to see me talking to a bunch of people, hopefully being very sincere and honest and emoting as I would. They're either going to like it or they're not. Really, all I've got to worry about is handling a nice hour of human relationships. All the other people will handle the TV show."

The very first Springer outing was a typical talk show "Reunion show" featuring Jane Purvis, a woman from Hamilton, Ohio, as a guest. As Jerry stood with his arms folded across his chest, politely listening, Jane tearfully explained that she had two children she had not seen for thirty-five years and was appearing on the show in hopes of being reunited with them at long last. "Talk some more," Jerry implored, obviously strip-mining for emotional gems as Jane dabbed at her teary eyes. "What's going on in your head now?"

But the tearful Purvis, seated on stage clutching the hand of her daughter Sandy, was so overwrought she could hardly speak. It was such an emotional moment, in fact, that many people in the audience were dabbing their eyes. Then, regaining her composure, Jane recalled for Jerry and the audience how in 1956 she had been shot six times by her husband, who had then fatally shot himself. And how a Georgia court had taken away her children, ages four years and four months, because she was hospitalized and had no income.

Suddenly a young man had stood up in the audience and asked, "Do you have any idea what your son looks like?" Then, before Jane could answer, the man cried, "Hi, Mom!" as the audience gasped. The two hugged on stage and Springer said, "Well, it's time to go to the Kleenex. We're going to take a break. We'll be right back."

After the show Springer slipped in behind Jane Purvis, her children, and four grandchildren, and urged viewers to reach out and touch a long-lost friend or relative. Then, looking into the camera, he told his audience, " 'Till next time, take care of yourself, and each other."

Three years later Jane Purvis took Jerry's advice. She took care of her second husband—shooting him to death in 1994 during a heated moment of spousal rage. Naturally when the Springer producers found out about Jane's tragic circumstances and her being imprisoned for murder, they were excited about the prospect of doing a retrospective program with her, especially since they had all that wonderful file footage of Jane's first appearance on Jerry's show. Unfortunately, perhaps mercifully, the state prison officials didn't think Jane should be on television. They denied the show access to Jane, and despite an ensuing flap from Springer's producers she remains in prison, far from the public eye, her television days only a distant, fading memory.

Jerry had been so convinced that the show would be a short-lived aberration in his normal routine he had failed to consider the toll doing a daily show would take. As a result he became a tornado of activity the first year his show was on the air. He was still co-anchoring the news with Norma Rashid three times a night and delivering his beloved commentaries when Multimedia announced in May, 1992, that the show would cease production on June 24 and, after a twelve week hiatus, resume production in Chicago. "Jerry will remain doing the news. We'll arrange a production schedule so he can stay on the air here," announced Burt Dubrow, the show's executive producer, adding, "at a minimum, it would seem to me that he could do four nights of news a week.

"The reason we're leaving," Dubrow explained, "has nothing to do with the city of Cincinnati. It has to do with getting guests. We love the audience here. We love the city. It's a tough decision, but it's what we have to do. It's impossible to do a major talk show anywhere but in a major city. The guests are not here. But they're always coming New York, Chicago or Los Angeles."

Actually, the move to Chicago was part of a $75 million package bought by NBC in a four-year contract to acquire Donahue, Sally Jessy Raphael, Rush Limbaugh, and Jerry Springer for its owned and operated stations. The move gave the Springer show better access to bigger guests and immediately pushed the show into more major markets—including New York, Chicago, Los Angeles, Philadelphia, San Francisco, Boston, Detroit, Washington, and Miami.

Thus began a tale of two cities. "I know I'm really lucky. I've got a national talk show, and tonight I'm getting on a plane to do the news. Still, I keep thinking, "Boy, one day, I'm really going to pay for all of this, you know?" Jerry conceded only a week after production had begun in Chicago. Only much later would he admit he'd been suffering from perpetual jet lag during those early months when he was commuting almost daily between the two cities.

By September, Springer had discovered he'd taken on a killer schedule, trying to do the Chicago show *and* the Cincinnati news. In fact, he would admit months later to a reporter, the first day he'd tried doing both jobs had wiped him out. "I came up here (to Chicago) at 7 A.M. which means I got up at 5:30 A.M. I did two shows, then got on a plane and went back to do the news in Cincinnati. By that time it was midnight and I had been up since 5:30 and I was jet-lagged twice. It's exhausting. It's very, very tiring," he told an interviewer.

Flying to Chicago had proven to usually be a breeze; but the drive from O'Hare Airport to downtown often took longer than the fifty-five-minute flight from Cincinnati. On several occasions Jerry had missed his flight back to Cincinnati due to bad weather or traffic congestion and had been unable to anchor the news. The stress of commuting was becoming a no joke situation. "Station executives," he joked, "are worried that I'm going to have a heart attack." Nevertheless he was determined not to give up either job. "That's my livelihood. I take it very seriously," he said of the newscast. "The truth is I love doing both, and I'm in no hurry to leave. I want to keep doing the news."

The *real* truth, however, was that Jerry was afraid to let go of the news job on the gamble that the talk show might turn out not to be a winner. "I wake up every morning thinking it will be my last show," he confided. "That's how I live my life. I've been on so many roller coasters, you know."

So, in a last ditch effort to hold onto his TV empire, Jerry decided to change his schedule. Instead of commuting daily, he would shoot two Jerry Springer shows on Saturday and do the other three by commuting two weekdays to Chicago. "To do it three days a week was silly," he explained, referring to his weekly commute between Cincinnati and Chicago.

Six months later, however, Jerry finally admitted to himself, and then to the WLWT-TV executives, that he could not continue the pace he had created for himself. "I thought I could do it, but I can't. I'm tired," he told them. "It's the right decision. I thought about it a lot over Christmas. I've tried to run back and read the news as often as I could but," he added, "nobody benefits from that—not me, the viewer, not anybody." He was relieved, and they were relieved by his decision because, in the intervening months that Jerry had been trying to do double duty, the station's news ratings had begun to fall. "I think I'm pictured now more as a talk show host than as a news anchor," he admitted. "I was at the station only three nights a week at best. And when you give people a chance to look elsewhere, they will."

Thus, in late January, 1993, Jerry relinquished his job as news anchorman. A month later he moved to Chicago. Although he knew he was going to miss Cincinnati, he felt comfortable taking up residence in the windy city because by then *The Jerry Springer Show* had expanded into a nationally syndicated show and was being carried on more than ninety stations, many of them major markets, around the country. "We've been given good time slots," Jerry excitedly told a friend. "We're not being buried in the middle of the night. It's one thing when it's in your hometown," he said of the show bearing his name. "But when it's in all these cities . . . it's like it's real!

"Last year," he continued, "I was saying the same thing, and believing it. But part of me was trying to convince myself as well as the press. Now we've reached the point where we're a show like everybody else."

As he bid *adieu* to Cincinnati Jerry had no idea he was in the beginning stages of a television career that would catapult him into an arena of outrage where he would be forced to endure "the slings and arrows of outrageous fortune" from a dizzying array of critics. All Jerry Springer knew in the early spring of 1993 was that he had a lucrative career, a binding contract, and the opportunity to make more money than he'd ever dreamed.

CHAPTER NINE

Life in the Fast Lane

"When you've got more than three million people in town, you're going to find at least a hundred and fifty who will come to anything."

Jerry Springer

Once settled in Chicago, Jerry was excited, elated, and somewhat apprehensive at being part of big time television. He was also amazed upon his arrival at the NBC Tower to discover his photo hanging on the lobby wall, alongside those of John Chancellor, Hugh Downs, Shelley Long, and Chicago personalities like Wild Kingdom's Marlin Perkins, and those stars of yesteryear, Mr. Wizard and Kukla, Fran & Ollie. And he was impressed to discover that his show was being taped just down the hall from *The Jenny Jones Show.*

He felt as if he had finally arrived, that the show was finally legitimate. "I think we're pretty close to getting some of the wives from the presidential race," he confided to a reporter in September, explaining, "before, we wouldn't even have had a return call. Now they are literally looking at tapes of the show. We are seriously on their list to have them as guests."

At that point, of course, the show had been seen in only a few markets, and Chicago was not one of them. As a result no one in the windy city had the slightest clue as to *who* Jerry Springer was. Thus, a month later, when a reporter paid a visit to the show there were only about "100 polite Midwesterners" in the audience and

Springer was filling the production lulls by doing Elvis
Presley impersonations in which he would turn up his
suit collar and croon "Love Me Tender". When nobody
swooned on this particular day, Springer suddenly
yelled "Elvis is alive! And he's in this building! Now
there's a show!" The audience laughed politely. They'd
only seen him in TV promotions for his show.

Although the show has always had an official "warm-
up guy," his duties mainly consist of telling the audience
what they can and cannot do during the taping—for instance, do not give the camera "the finger" and do not
storm the stage. It's Springer who truly warms up the
crowd, suddenly appearing from the wings, grabbing the
mike, and launching into a string of Borscht Belt jokes
like "My best friend ran off with my wife. . . ." Pause.
". . . I really miss him."

Jerry has always worked his audiences. On his first
syndicated show from Cincinnati, he'd entertained
that audience of 150 people by doing a stiff imitation
of Phil Donahue. In Chicago it was Elvis imitations.
"My political life has always been shaking hands, working the crowd, the interplay," he's said on many occasions. "The fact is, I love working the crowd. What
made me nervous was having that camera, an inani-
mate object, on me and trying to relate to people at
the same time."

This penchant for interplay explains why Springer
has always posed for photographs with his guests and
audience members, and always shakes hands with every
guest and every audience member after each taping.
Only then does he disappear into his office down the
hall from the studio, where tufts of freshly pulled hair
usually can be found on the green carpet stage, rem-
nants of yet another highly-charged Springer outing.

* * *

Despite his lack of notoriety, Jerry was obviously happy. He compared Chicagoans to Cincinnati folks, saying, "Everybody here is very nice. They were friendly in the audience, particularly when you consider that we're not on the air here yet. There is an openness here which is a lot like Cincinnati."

He also appeared unconcerned that his audiences had been sparse, and that the studio hadn't been filled during his first week's worth of tapings. "In a city this size, it has nothing to do with whether the show is good or bad," he explained. "When you've got more than three million in town, you're going to find at least a hundred and fifty who will come to anything."

Even after his move from Cincinnati to Chicago Jerry continued to work at a breakneck pace, pouring all of his energies into the show, leaving no time for anything resembling what most people would consider to be "a life." Having given up the job security of doing the news for a decade, he was running scared, whether he knew it or not, taping two shows a day and spending his weekends flying around the country, promoting the show in major markets like New York, Detroit, and Washington, and constantly taping promotional spots: "Hi, this is Jerry Springer. My Northwestern University professors warned me years ago that I'd never make it as a lawyer. They were right. So I got this talk show, and I hope you come and see it." Plus he was also trying to make time for his daughter Katie, often flying her into Chicago for the weekend.

At that point Jerry was taping five shows Monday through Wednesday, jetting out of Chicago on Wednesday night, returning early Saturday morning, resting on Sunday, and then repeating the process all over again. He was also rising at 3 A.M. to do morning radio, news-

In 1970, a young Jerry Springer campaigned, unsuccessfully, for Congress as a Democrat. © 1970/*Cincinnati Enquirer*

Jerry managed to be re-elected to the Cincinnati city council in 1975, even after publicly admitting he had enjoyed the services of a Kentucky prostitute and paid her with a personal check.
© 1976/Cincinnati Enquirer

As newly elected mayor of Cincinnati, Jerry basks in the glow of victory with vice mayor J. Kenneth Blackwell.
© 1977/Cincinnati Enquirer

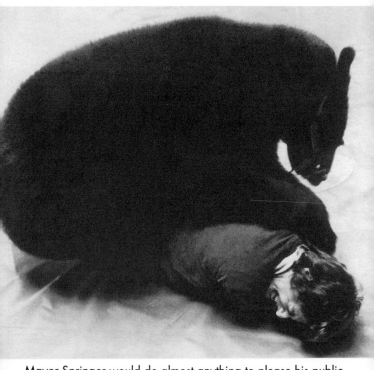

Mayor Springer would do almost anything to please his public, even wrestle bears! © 1980/Cincinnati Enquirer

Born in 1976 to Jerry and his wife Micki, daughter Katie is the love of his life. © 1982/Cincinnati Enquirer

Now all grown up, Katie and dad Jerry are extremely close. She recently visited him at WMAQ studios in Chicago. © 1998/Cincinnati Enquirer

As a news anchor and political commentator for WLWT-TV in Cincinnati, Jerry was tremendously well-liked and respected. © *Globe Photos, Inc./1991*

Jerry loosens his tie to launch his talk show in 1991—little did anyone suspect that a few years later, it would devolve into a virtual amateur boxing match and rocket to the top of the ratings. © *Globe Photos, Inc./1991*

A billboard promoting the show in 1994, the turning point
when Jerry made a savvy decision to go beyond the mere
dysfunctional, and boldly dive straight into the gutter
with the most explosive guests he could find.
Jason Trigg/Archive Photos/1994

Jerry has hit the big time, shown here in 1994 with Phil
Donahue, Ernie Anastos and Rush Limbaugh.
© 1994/Andrea Ranault/Globe Photos, Inc.

Jerry returns to his political roots at the 1996 Democratic
Convention. After graduating from law school, Jerry had
worked as an aide to Robert F. Kennedy.
Ron Sachs/CNP/Archive Photos/1996

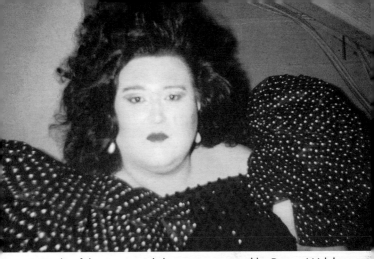

A staple of the revamped show were guests like Denny Welch, a.k.a. Eartha Quake, the 800-pound drag queen shown here in full regalia. *Courtesy of Denny Welch*

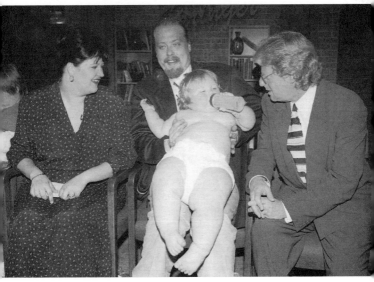

At 17 months old, Zack Strenkert weighed in at a freakish 70 pounds. Jerry arranged for a genetic specialist to try to cure the tot's obesity. *© 1996/Michael Kardis/AP/Wide World Photos*

Jerry playfully tries to muzzle his TV-persona in an unwitting
display of ambivalence about his role as the Sultan of Sleaze.
© 1996/Ed Geller/Globe Photos, Inc.

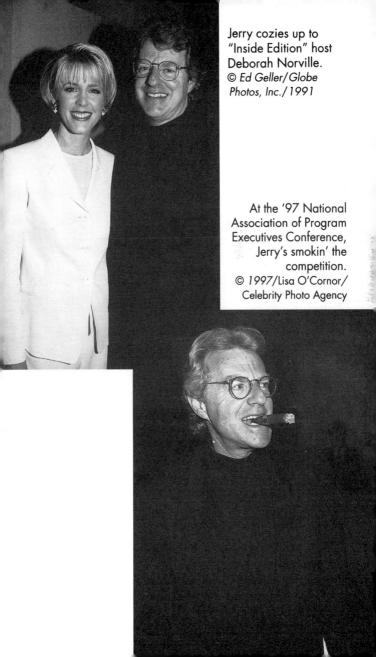

Jerry cozies up to "Inside Edition" host Deborah Norville.
© Ed Geller/Globe Photos, Inc./1991

At the '97 National Association of Program Executives Conference, Jerry's smokin' the competition.
© 1997/Lisa O'Cornor/ Celebrity Photo Agency

Popular comedian Steve Harvey had Jerry on his show in 1997. © 1997/Fitzroy Barrett/Globe Photos, Inc.

Jerry gets down, singing with the band The Rattled Roosters at
the trendy Viper Room in L.A. Jerry tried, with little success,
to launch a career as a country singer with the release of his
CD "Dr. Talk." *1994/Reuters/Fred Prouser/Archive Photos*

With the #1-rated show and bestselling video, former Cincinnati mayor and 'serious' journalist Springer is laughing all the way to the bank. © AP/Wide World *Photos*

Jerry kicks back in his Chicago condo, overlooking downtown
and Lake Michigan. © 1997/Cincinnati Enquirer

Before taping a show featuring pregnant strippers, Jerry warms up the crowd. © 1997/Cincinnati Enquirer

paper, and TV interviews, as well as station promotions and sales receptions. "It's like I'm running for president," he told a reporter in 1993. "It's a national campaign. Every Thursday and Friday I'm on the road. This is a competitive business, and I'm not staying on the air because I'm good-looking or have this great talent. We hustle. In every market, you have to campaign hard."

As a result of this hectic, non-stop schedule, six months after he'd moved to Chicago Jerry was still living in his six-room, one-and-a-half bath Michigan Avenue area apartment under less than homey conditions.

A visitor to Jerry's apartment in November, 1993, for instance, recalls being surprised upon realizing there were only four glasses and a few dishes in the kitchen, and that the food in the refrigerator consisted solely of a half gallon of sour milk, a candy bar, and a bottle of mineral water.

Price stickers were still pasted on the toothbrush holder and soap dish in the bathroom, only one shelf in the linen closet was filled, price tags were still hanging off some of the living room furniture, and a cluster of still unhung pictures were propped against a bedroom wall. And there were no curtains at the windows. "Hey, I'm a guy." Jerry had shrugged. "It's just a guy's place, a place to hang out," he said, explaining, "I buy things in clusters. This is how I live. I don't care about stuff. I don't cook, I eat out every night. So I don't need anything in the kitchen. The Restaurant Association should give me an award!"

Then he proudly explained how he'd furnished the apartment in a whirlwind shopping spree during an hour-and-a-half lunch break from the show. "I'd had lunch at one of my favorite restaurants and I had an hour and a half to spare before taping the show. So I thought, 'Okay, I need some stuff, a place to sit.' So I stopped at Crate & Barrel and bought everything. The saleslady could probably send her kid to college after that day."

Jerry had found his first Chicago apartment in much the same way—by happenstance and need. "If I had to pick the defining block in Chicago this would be it. So I walked into this building because it was on this block and they had an apartment for rent. I didn't expect to come back and be able to look out at Lake Michigan from my office window," he said, adding, "from here you can see the lake and the whole city."

Five years and many millions of dollars later, Jerry lives an even higher life, literally. His home is now a condo on the ninety-first floor of the John Hancock Center, with an even more spectacular view of The Loop, Chicago's famous Navy Pier, and Lake Michigan for as far as the eye can see. In his free time, which is minimal, Springer spends time with his daughter, plays golf, attends virtually all of the Chicago Bulls' home games, and hangs out with the guys. He is still interested in reading political histories, and his conversation leans more toward baseball and his political heroes, Franklin D. Roosevelt and the Kennedy brothers. Like his heroes, he is also an avid cigar smoker.

"My first experience with cigars was in college. I had a roommate thirty years ago at Tulane University whose father was in the cigar business. That was my first introduction to cigars and I really enjoyed them. But then I just kind of dropped it. I was never much of a smoker of any sort until a few years ago I started smoking cigars again. I do look forward to smoking a great cigar," he admits, adding, "I smoke three or four a week now. When I go out at night for a nice dinner I want to know in advance that I have a cigar to look forward to after eating.

"I smoke mostly Ashtons or Davidoffs; but, at this

point, if someone gives me a cigar and says, 'try this, it's great,' I have to give it a try. I'm in the process of saving labels now. So if I find something new, the next time I go out I'll get those. I'm not such a connoisseur that I won't say I won't have this, I won't have that; but I've got a humidor now so I'm into the whole bit."

As for the condo furnishings? Well, at least the price tags are gone.

Within a year of Jerry's move to the windy city television had suddenly become glutted with syndicated talk shows, all of them spewing forth information on every conceivable subject. Geraldo. Jenny Jones. Montel Williams. Phil Donahue. Sally Jessy Raphael. And, at the head of the list, Oprah Winfrey, The Diva of Daytime, who was *always* first in the ratings. TV talk shows were coming and going so rapidly that no one, not even the nation's television critics, could keep track of who was where and what was what. So it was a big surprise when a year old talk show hosted by a twenty-seven-year-old actress named Ricki Lake landed in second place, seemingly overnight, during one of the industry's ratings "sweep" weeks.

Considering that Lake's only prior claim to fame had been her film debut in *Hairspray,* a 1988 John Waters cult comedy, and an amazing ability to sustain her acting career by portraying overweight, frequently neurotic, best friends and sidekicks, the swift success of her show was even more astonishing. Within months of her 1993 debut, Lake had found her place in TV history as The Sweetheart of Generation X by offering her viewers a daily diet of such titillating subjects as "Girlfriend, I Slept With Your Man and I'll Do It Again" and moments like this:

Ed had told his side of the story, and now Tasha was telling hers.

"He's mine. She has to deal with that now," Tasha was saying. Tasha, married to Ed, was angry with Becky, Ed's ex-girlfriend, who she believed was trying to come between them. When Tasha's story wound down Becky came on stage, and the situation began to really heat up.

"Well, to begin with they done nothin' but lie since they been up here," Becky said. She was in the midst of explaining the lies when Tasha suddenly leaped to her feet. With the studio audience roaring, the two women began screaming at each other, nose to nose, fingers on all four hands jabbing the air, while the bleep machine struggled to keep up. The confrontation ended with a high decibel exchange of "Shut up!" "You shut up!"

Enter Ricki Lane. "Excuse me, excuse me," she interrupted, jumping up on stage. "We don't say 'shut up' to anyone. This is an open arena. We will all be heard, and we won't use the bad language, okay?"

If this all sounds too familiar it's because it is—now. Ricki Lake had enormous impact on the content of daytime talk shows. Within months of her show's 1993 debut she had forever changed the tenor, tone, and topics of syndicated gabfests. With her meteoric rise in popularity, newcomers and old competitors alike soon gravitated toward her high-pitched style and subject matter like moths to ratings flames. Among them was Jerry Springer, a *mensch* about to become a *meister* of the worst kind of *schlock*.

CHAPTER TEN

Low Road, High Ratings

"This is America, and everyone's entitled to share the microphone."

Jerry Springer

In early 1994, despite all of his hard work during the previous year, Jerry's worst fears had become a reality: *The Jerry Springer Show* was on the ropes. Jerry and the show's producers had been told by Multimedia executives that if the Springer show ratings didn't drastically improve by the end of November, 1994, they were going to cancel the program.

Jerry had known he wasn't a ratings winner—not up against such formidable competition as Ricki and Jenny and Sally—but he was still shocked to hear Multimedia was actually serious about canceling his show. It was obvious something needed to be done, and done quickly. But what?

Enter Richard Dominick, the show's new executive producer. *He* knew what needed to be done. He just wasn't sure that Jerry would go along with it.

One night Dominick invited Springer to dinner. Afterward the two men took a long walk down Michigan Avenue. When they returned to the studio the die had been cast. The Springer show was going to change drastically—and quickly. No more reunion shows. No more politicians. No authors. Definitely no sociologists, psychologists, or for that matter, anthropologists. And no more Mr. Nice Guy. Nudity, sex, bizarre relationships, transsexuals, teenage strippers, and Ku Klux Klan members became the battle cry for the May, 1994, ratings. And it worked.

"We made it wild in ninety-four," Dominick would later crow. "That's when I told Jerry, 'Put away the issues. Let Ted Koppel do the issues at night. Let's not save the world. We are television!'" Most insiders now credit the Springer show's miraculous, albeit sleazy, turn around to Dominick, not only because he is the show's executive producer but because he has a background befitting the current climate of the show. The forty-five-year-old New Jersey native once made a living writing stories and headlines—"Three Month Old Baby Speaks!" "Toaster Possessed by Devil!"—for newspapers like *The Weekly World News,* a raunchy tabloid who specializes in alien abductions, three-headed babies and other incredible tales from the land beyond reason. This fact, however, is not mentioned in Dominick's *official* Springer show biography.

Instead, the bio concentrates on Dominick's television background, which includes a stint as an on-air investigative reporter for the *Wilson North Report,* a late night comedy show which lasted less than a blink, and an equally brief stint as a producer for the NBC comedy series, *House Party.* He then created the first three episodes of *Cape Bongo,* a comedy/horror anthology supposedly *still* being considered for production by Nickelodeon. He was the sole writer for ESPN's 1991 *Sports Emmy Awards* hosted by comic Dennis Miller. That same year Dominick moved to Chicago and joined *The Jerry Springer Show* as a producer. Since then he's had a meteoric rise within the organization, moving first to coordinating producer and then in 1993 to senior producer and finally, in May, 1994, to the exalted position of executive producer. The rest, as the cliché goes, is history—a history that Dominick loves recalling for anyone who inquires.

"It just wasn't working," he says of the show. "Nobody was watching. When I came in as executive producer Multimedia said, you have until November to get ratings or the show is cancelled. So me (sic) and Jerry decided that to survive we needed to go after what we called The Letterman Crowd. If we could get college kids interested in the show and get some kind of cult following we could survive. So we changed the show immediately from an issue oriented show to a spectacle." But not the spectacle it is today. That wouldn't occur until after November, 1996, when Universal Television purchased the rights to the Springer show in a $50 million deal that also included the Sally Jessy Raphael and the now-cancelled Pat Bullard talk shows, the international syndication rights of Donahue, and several other programs. Until then *The Jerry Springer Show* content had been heavily edited by its previous two owners—Multimedia and Gannett—for violence, obscenities, and nudity. Both Dominick claims, had been very conservative and had therefore kept the show under very tight control.

"Every time we'd push the envelope," he says, "they'd say 'Pull back, pull back! Tone it down.' We've always done a wild show. Fights were breaking out all the time. I used to bring friends to the show being taped, and they'd invariably say 'What a great show!' Then they'd see it on television three weeks later, and say 'Gee, when I saw it, it was a lot different.' And I'd say 'That was because we had to cut so much out.' "

Then along came Universal Television and everything changed, from the bleeps to the violence. "When Universal bought us in 1996, they said, 'Do your show, just do your show. We'll worry about everything else,' " says Dominick, adding that was when he told the show's producers, "If the show's not interesting with the sound off, don't bring it to me. What we needed to do," he adds, "was get people as they were surfing the channels so at whatever moment they hit our show they would find it interesting."

In January, 1997, Dominick once again changed the show's format with Universal's approval and blessings. "They came to us and asked what we could do to break out of the pack. I said, 'Let us show what really goes on.' They said 'Okay, do it.'"

It was then that *The Jerry Springer Show* fully underwent the transformation that has turned it into the freak show it has become today. When the executives at Universal didn't bother to pick up the phone to complain about the show's increasingly raunchy and violent content, Dominick knew he had a winner and he added a couple of extra flourishes to the format, like the informative "what's happening" captions. Not only do the captions let channel surfing viewers know what's going on within seconds of tuning in, they assist the audience already tuned in in understanding what is happening during the bleeped out slugfests as well.

The strategy worked. The numbers have climbed quickly and steadily. Jerry Springer, ignoring those who thought he was sullying his image and previous accomplishments by wallowing in televised garbage, has become a household name, thanks to episodes like "Pimps vs. Prostitutes!" and "I'm Here to Steal Your Lover!"

"Now you're seeing it in all its glory," Dominick was triumphantly telling his friends by early Spring 1997.

It was around the same time that, in a moment of capitalistic genius, Dominick realized there was a fortune to be made from the segments that were too raunchy to be aired even on the *new* Jerry Springer show. It would be a simple matter, he reasoned, to exhume clips from past shows and edit them into a series of video-tapes. It was brilliant. It was easy. It was, as it turned out, a gold mine.

Titled *TOO HOT FOR TV!* the tape, which consists of fifty-four minutes of unbridled, unbleeped, uncensored nudity, obscenity, and unbelievable hijinks, was released in October, 1997, and quickly became the fastest selling TV title in the history of home video. It was an amazing feat, since the video has been too hot for television, and too hot for video stores, and therefore has been available only by mail order. So far that hasn't held the viewing public back from telephoning in a half-million orders of the $19.95 tape. It's also not surprising that the video has become a smash hit on the party circuit, thanks to segments such as "My Sister Slept with My Three Husbands," "I'm Proud to Be a Racist" and "Holiday Hell with My Feuding Family."

Now, for the same price, there's an entire series of TOO HOT tapes—Too Hot For TV Secrets, Too Hot For TV Surprises and Too Hot For TV Wild Relationships—containing uncensored scenes of everything from buck-naked men and women to people spewing purple prose and profanity, as well as a TOO HOT DELUXE video which boasts "all-new bonus footage" for an extra ten dollars, plus postage and handling, of course. And there's more to come, like Too Hot For TV: Bad Boys and Naughty Girls, which will be released in August. The supply, as anyone who's ever watched the show realizes by now, is unlimited.

"We can't believe how well the tape is doing," acknowledged Darren Howell, a spokesperson for Real Entertainment, the Santa Monica, California, company distributing the Springer tapes. "It looks like it will outpace 'Cops: Too Hot to Handle for TV,' and that video has sold more than three million."

According to Howell, not everyone calling up to order the tape is simply an unknown viewer from Tiny Town, USA, either. Howell said there have been a surprising number of celebrities dialing the 800 number, including superstar basketball player Charles Barkley, hip hop king Sean "Puff Daddy" Combs and Roseanne, as well as basketball star Shaquille O'Neal. Even director Quentin Tarantino's office once called, but not about acquiring a copy of the video. Tarantino was interested in possibly recruiting frequent Springer guest Danny the Wonder Pony, a guy who saddles himself up and then gives piggyback rides to squealing women, for a small role in one of his films.

"The tapes," claim Howell, "have become bigger than the show!"

And where does Jerry Springer fit into all this? Well, for starters, he ends each of the TOO HOT tapes with a Final Disclaimer, no doubt originally penned on a yellow legal pad, in an amusing attempt to somehow distance himself from the perversion and purple prose contained in each of the videos. "Please understand," he explains, "that because we show it does not constitute an endorsement of it, any more than reporting a murder on the news or a prime-time movie about a rape is an endorsement of those horrors." As for deriving great revenue from the sales of the tapes, Laurie Fried, a publicist for the Springer Show, claims Springer only receives "a flat, minimal fee" for his services and earns no profit from the sales. If that is indeed true, Jerry should find himself a new agent—immediately. According to Darren Howell, Real Entertainment is launching a mass marketing effort to have the X-rated tapes available in retail stores as well as porn shops this summer and is expecting Springer to travel the country doing personal appearances. "We want to offer our customers Jerry Springer in any form," says Howell.

However, the company recently began a national television campaign to hawk the videos by running ads not only on the Springer show, but on *Sally Jessy Raphael, E! Entertainment,* and the USA Network, all of which are conveniently either produced or owned by Universal Television, and Jerry was nowhere to be found.

CHAPTER ELEVEN

All Action, No Talk

"I'll sign on the dotted line that this is the silliest, craziest show on television, and at times, it's just plain stupid."

Jerry Springer

In 1995, *The Jerry Springer Show* took a huge ratings leap forward and exalted in having mostly scantily clad women and teenage and transsexual strippers as program guests. In 1996, however, Dominick reported there would be a change in format. "This year," he announced to the media, "all of my guests have their clothes on." The reason for this shift in clothing turned out to be because, unless you're a Sumo wrestler it's just too difficult to punch, push, poke, and fight when you're naked. However, during one show featuring nudists and titled "I Refuse to Wear Clothes" there did turn out to be a typical Springer show slugfest. In that incident, though, the two naked female guests simply sat in their chairs, legs appropriately, demurely crossed, and watched as their fully clothed boyfriends got into a fight. "We don't want nice, we want spice," wrote a TV reviewer, aghast at what he had witnessed.

As it quickly became apparent, 1996 was to become "The Year of the Fight" on the Springer show, thanks to heartwarming programs like "Christmas with the Klan" and "Incest Family," the brainchild of twenty-eight-year-old producer Brenda You, who is noted for religiously scouring the American and British tabloids in pursuit of strange and bizarre subjects to be translated into Springer show fodder. When one reporter visited backstage at the show, for example, You was busily trying to track down a male college professor who had been fired for teaching class in a skirt and high heels according to a *National Enquirer* article.

Mothers against daughters, husbands against wives, siblings squared off against each other. With the format change green lighted by Universal, *The Jerry Springer Show* suddenly became something akin to televised wrestling in front of a booing, cheering, jeering, frenetic crowd. The only elements missing were the mats, the ropes, and any defined rules of grappling. As for a referee, there has never actually been one. Most of the time Springer observes the violent outbursts that have become the hallmark of his show from afar.

"Normally, if you watch closely," he points out, "I'm never anywhere near the fights. I'm pretty much of a chicken. I always stand near the crowd. I'm afraid once I get into it I'll never get away from it. Sometimes it looks as if it's going to be obvious. I know as much as the audience does. When you have two guys fighting over the same girl and one has been trashing the other, you know the other guy isn't going to be too happy. Sometimes you just get the feeling, just being able to read the body language."

However, not long ago there was an exception to this Springer Golden Rule. Jerry did get involved—too much, according to Dominick—and as a result the show may never air. What happened is pure Jerry Springer:

A man named Dennis wanted to reconcile with his wife, Liz, for the sake of the couple's three children, and wound up in fisticuffs with her boyfriend, Dave. Everything was going along *fightingly* well until Liz revealed she had allowed Dennis to move back into the family home because he had attempted to commit suicide, a fact the show's producers had not known. As Liz continued to berate Dennis he appeared to become increasingly upset until, finally, Jerry could stand it no more. He went up on stage, sat between the twosome, congratulated Liz for allowing Dennis to return home, and advised Dennis to concentrate more on helping himself than retrieving his relationship with Liz.

The segment represented two problems for the producers. First of all, had they known about the suicide attempt they would not have allowed the trio on the program because they do not book guests with severe psychological difficulties, a situation they attempt to screen out by interviewing guests at least three times prior to booking them. Secondly, Dominick was displeased with Jerry suddenly becoming involved as an on stage participant during the taping. Although it was a poignant moment, he explained afterward, "That's not our show." Indeed, poignancy is definitely not a quality the show pursues. Outrage, that's what the show is seeking.

"The only thing we work at (to make our show unique) is to make sure it is outrageous," Jerry has repeatedly explained. "We've become, for better or worse, the symbol of the crazy talk show. It's silly, stupid, crazy, outrageous entertainment. And as soon as people realize what it is, they figure out if they want to choose to watch it." He was, at the time, headed into the studio to tape a show called "Stop Sleeping with My Lover!" Just as he reached the door, he turned and, as an afterthought, added, "It's a cartoon. That's what we are. There are political cartoons; we are a social cartoon."

The show actually is all about the crowd. Springer paces up and down the aisles throughout the tapings, giving the appearance of interacting with the audience while at the same time remaining aloof from it. And the studio audience, rarely ever given the opportunity to ask questions, is actually little more than a rooting section—for the host. "Jerr-eee! Jerr-eee!" they yell whenever a fight breaks out. "I don't know where that came from, when it started," he conceded during a recent appearance on *The RuPaul Show.* "And I don't know why they yell my name. I'm not going to get in a fight!"

The show's format is always the same. The guests seem hand-picked for their confrontational personalities. Guests who should be separated are seated next to each other so that when they begin their inevitable screaming and shoving matches the camera crew can easily, swiftly catch every sensationalistic moment of the action. The same is true as the security men rush on stage to pull the warring factions apart. They, too, become fodder for the camera. Later, in the editing room, the show will be put together with shots of the guests, the audience, the bouncers and, of course, Jerry Springer—compiled and inter-cut with an eye to the show's best tawdry interests.

Safely tucked in the midst of his audience, Springer adds a certain flavor to the show by asking leading questions designed to feed the chaos; and by dispensing odd bits of sophomoric philosophy such as: "If a man tells another man to kick a pregnant woman in the stomach so she'll lose her baby, he's not a good father." Shades of that wise detective of yore, Charlie Chan! His films were peppered with equally wise sayings, like *"It is difficult to pick up needle with boxing glove"* and *"Bad alibi like dead fish—cannot stand test of time."* Or perhaps, as in the case of Jerry Springer, "Tongue often hang man quicker than rope!"

Occasionally, however, Springer *does* find himself too close to the stage when asking a question that creates spontaneous combustion among his guests. At those moments of suddenly ignited violence, Springer has tried to defuse the situation, sometimes successfully, sometimes not, with the admonishment: "Don't get up while I'm standing here 'cause . . . I'M SCARED!" An interviewer once asked Springer, tongue in cheek, why he didn't just put his guests in glass isolation booths. Springer laughed, then responded, "Because glass is so expensive and broken glass is *awful!*"

In the years since *The Jerry Springer Show* switched from limp to lascivious, its host has created an intriguing philosophy concerning the program's circus-like content and his center stage position as ringmaster. "My job," he explains, "is to make sure the microphone is there, even for people whose views I despise. I can put up with the notion of having Ku Klux Klan or neo-Nazi pigs on my show because the only way to deal with racism is to expose it. When you see these clowns in their sheets and uniforms you see how absurd and hateful they are. It's when we censor it that it becomes dangerous."

Nevertheless, as it turns out, the only guest to ever truly upset Springer happened to be a guy in a white sheet. Jerry remembers the occasion well. The guy was a member of the Ku Klux Klan and, as Springer recalls, "Throughout the whole show he kept referring to me as 'you hook-nosed Jew bastard.' I never got upset; I just thought he was an idiot. But then he started talking about my mom, and I kinda lost it—which was stupid of me. I mean, these people are on the show because they're outrageous, so I shouldn't get personally upset because they *are* outrageous. I have to be big enough to say, 'I hate what you say, but I'll fight to the death for your right to say it.' "

Since Jerry's guests tend to be working class, often uneducated and inarticulate people, the odds are enormously against there being any provocative thoughts displayed during the hour. Greatly increasing those odds is the fact that any emotional issues explored, if

you can call it that, are examined before a loudly booing, hissing, cheering, or clapping studio audience. It
is a volcano of pent-up anguish just waiting to explode.
And it usually does.

As the show's topics have grown increasingly raunchy
and the guests have become more prone to violence, the
audiences have also gotten progressively wilder. It is a
sordid combination that nevertheless has allowed the
show's ratings to make a significant, amazing leap forward in the past two years. And although both Springer
and his producer, Dominick, insist they do not promote
the fighting, that they try to stop it as fast as it occurs,
the show's increased ratings can only be attributed to
the sporadic fighting that punctuates each and every
Springer outing.

Carefully crafted to bring out the worst in its guests,
the show unfailingly manipulates the situation, whether
it involves angry family members, spurned lovers, or
white supremacists. This is accomplished by bringing
out the guests in stages and then seating the feuding
factions next to each other or, at the very least, in close
punching proximity. Moreover, guests are brought out
in stages, so that the guest who has had an affair with
a married woman is asked to remain seated as the cuck-
old husband makes his entrance. More often than not
the offended third party will appear from out of nowhere, storm the stage, and head straight for his or her
adversary with arms swinging and mouth cursing, and
the guest is quickly pummeled, much to the delight of
the studio audience. In this devious manner, confrontations are not only permitted they're encouraged. And
they've escalated.

Take, for example, the December, 1997, show titled
"You won't Ruin My Relationship." That particular
Springer outing featured two women fighting over the
same man, pouncing on each other, fists and tufts of

hair flying, seven times in one segment. It took four security guards as well as several crew members to repeatedly separate them—but not until the audience's taste for violence had been mostly satisfied.

"It goes in cycles," Springer says of the increased violence. "Now everyone who comes on is someone who has watched the show and has called up. It has now become the thing to do. They see everyone else on the shows fighting, so when they come on and they get angry, they figure it's okay. Now they all do it. In response to that we now have cops up there."

True. However, as one newspaper reviewer wrote, "those security guys of his are the slowest moving humans since Tim Conway's old man character on 'The Carol Burnett Show.'"

Steve Wilkos would take umbrage at the thought that he and his staff were not responding quickly enough to the ever-erupting melees on the show. Big, bald-headed and tough as nails, the six foot, three-inch thirty-two-year-old Wilkos is head of security for *The Jerry Springer Show,* a moonlighting job he's held since 1993. He is also a patrolman with the Chicago Police Department and works in one of the city's toughest neighborhoods, The 14th District, *aka* The Shakespeare District.

With his shaved head and muscular physique, Wilkos is difficult to miss and even harder to forget when he jumps up on stage and pulls guests apart, sometimes one with each of his muscular arms. Wilkos and his staff of six, off-duty, Chicago cops and the show's stage manager who doubles as a security guard are always positioned at the base of the stage, out of the eye of the camera, waiting and ready to break up the skirmishes that punctuate the program. Since 1997, they've been getting all the action they can handle.

"I think the shows we're doing now are just a little different than we used to do," Wilkos concedes. "We used to do a lot of reunion shows, makeover shows, and we're not doing that anymore. I don't think we are doing anything to cause fights; I just think the topics of the show are getting people riled up." And, Wilkos admits, even though he sometimes has to hurl himself into the middle of as many as six or seven fights per show, working on the Springer show is great, challenging fun. He and his staff use different techniques to subdue guests, depending on whether the aggressor is a man or a woman. For example, they invariably disable angry male guests by grabbing them from behind and pushing them down. If a woman gets out of hand, they stop her by squeezing her wrists to prevent the usual hair pulling. The shows featuring fighting transsexuals are the worst, says Wilkos, because "they can throw punches *AND* pull hair!" During *those* tapings the number of security guards is increased.

On those particular shows Steve spends so much of his time up on stage separating the more violence-prone guests that once, during a show featuring several battling transvestites, his parents tuned in, saw him on stage, and got confused. "They called and said, 'You're not gay, are you?' " he laughingly recalled.

Despite the ongoing outbursts on the Springer show, Wilkos still finds "The real life police stuff is actually more dangerous. You never know what's going to happen. Here," he explains, "we know what's going to happen. Someone might throw a punch, pull some hair, and we get up there and break it up. Nobody ever gets seriously hurt, and nobody has ever really hassled us." Nevertheless, security staff members have still endured bruised shins, cuts, and sprains. One melee even led one guard to suffer a painful pulled groin.

When it comes to obscenities, however, the only way the Springer show has to guard against broadcasting the seemingly unending cursing is the ability to bleep out the foul words. And bleep they do—often to the extent that several minutes pass without one discernible word being heard by the home audience. "The guests shout so many bleeped obscenities," proffered one newspaper columnist, "that the show sounds like a test of the emergency broadcast system."

Springer has an interesting, philosophical argument for the foul language huffed and puffed on stage by his guests. "Culture is changing," he says. "Words which two generations ago we thought were foul have now become very much a part of the language. My guess is that twenty or thirty years from now words we consider vulgar today won't be vulgar then. In other words, language is always a growing process of change. In the beginning it is a shock value. Today you would not be offended if I said, 'What the hell is going on here?' But, the truth is, you would have been kicked out of your church if you'd said that twenty years ago.

"So," he concludes, "it's important to recognize that with language, even though we bleep out now what is offensive, is a fluid thing, that it's always changing, and that we don't grow up being worse people because we heard a bad word."

Of course, this is the same guy who, when asked what he liked best about being a talk show host, replied, "The idea that every day is totally different and that I meet fascinating people whom I might never run into otherwise. I get up in the morning and I know it's going to be an exciting day."

CHAPTER TWELVE

Sex, Lies and Video

"They (the guests) are absolutely told ahead of time what the possibilities of the secret could be. They are not blindsided. They don't come on thinking, 'Oh, great, it's going to be a show about dancing.'"

Jerry Springer

In March, 1995, Jonathan Schmitz, a twenty-four-year-old waiter from a suburban Detroit area appeared as a guest on the Chicago-based *Jenny Jones Show* in a program titled "Secret Admirers," a theme that had been used in the past and had proven to be a hit with the audience. But this time it took a tragic turn.

Prior to agreeing to be a panelist on the show, Schmitz reportedly had inquired whether his secret admirer was a woman. To which a Jones show producer allegedly had replied it might be a man or it might be a woman. Thus it wasn't until the cameras were rolling before the studio audience that Schmitz discovered *his* "secret admirer" was none other than his gay neighbor, thirty-two-year-old Scott Amedure. Although he seemed stunned and a little embarrassed, Schmitz handled the surprise with a certain aplomb, telling the audience he was "flattered" by Amedure's implied offer to enter into a closer relationship with him. But he had quickly added, "I'm heterosexual."

After the taping Schmitz, Amedure, and a woman friend went out together for a night out on the town complete with dinner and drinks, compliments of *The Jenny Jones Show.* End of story? Not by a long shot.

Three days after he'd returned to Detroit from the Chicago taping, Schmitz decided to go shopping. First he went to a sporting goods store, where he purchased a shotgun. Then he went to a second store and bought some ammunition. Next, with his purchases in hand, Schmitz dropped by Amedure's trailer home, and when Amedure answered the door he shot him twice in the chest at almost point blank range, killing him instantly. Then Schmitz went home, where he was quickly arrested. Questioned by police as to his motive, Schmitz said he had felt humiliated by what had happened on the Jones show and it had "eaten away" at him. He blamed Amedure whom he believed, he told his interrogators, had "fucked me on national TV."

Jenny Jones expressed sympathy for both the dead man and the Schmitz family but denied that he had been misled. "As much as we all regret what happened," she said, "the fact is this tragedy is about the actions of one individual." Most of her colleagues in the world of talk agreed with her. Some of the news media also concurred. "We're all responsible for what we do," said former CBS news correspondent Marvin Kalb. "It becomes too much of a cop-out for anyone to claim that it was a television talk show that was principally responsible for a dreadful action." Not everyone agreed, however.

As would be expected there was an immediate hue and cry from the public, the media, even a number of government officials, most of whom blamed *The Jenny Jones Show,* along with talk shows in general, for having created an atmosphere that would ultimately lead to murder.

One of the most vociferous voices railing against the excessive violence and nudity found on daytime televi-

sion talk shows in the aftermath of the Amedure shooting was William Bennett, the former U.S. education secretary. Firmly convinced that shows like those hosted by
Jenny Jones and, especially Jerry Springer, had crossed
the line of acceptability, Bennett, along with Democratic
Senators Joseph Lieberman and Sam Nunn, launched a
crusade against so-called "Trash TV" in October, 1995.
Through Empower America, a conservative public interest group claiming to have more than 400,000 members,
the threesome lashed out at all of the nation's sleazier
talk shows, but focused most of their attention on the
Springer show, citing it as a main contributor to "pervasive cultural rot" in America. "These shows increasingly make the abnormal normal and set up the most
perverse role models," Bennett said during a press conference. "It's time for a revolt of the revolted!"

"Today," Bennett announced, "we declare ourselves
to be part of a resistance, a resistance operation to the
giant popular-culture sleaze machine."

Springer saw a politically motivated conservative plot
forming right before his bespectacled eyes and quickly
launched a counterattack, defending his show somewhat in the manner of David squaring off in front of
Goliath. "There is a kind of elitism in this whole issue,"
Springer told the members of the media, all of whom
dutifully recorded his words. "Powerful people are on
TV all the time and as long as they speak the King's
English we say it's okay. But then you get someone who
isn't wealthy, who doesn't have a title or position, and
they come on and talk about something that's important to them—and all of a sudden we call that trash."

The fact that Bennett's objection to programs such
as the Springer show had nothing to do with class struggle but everything to do with content and behavior was
neatly deflected, hidden away in the carefully crafted
rhetoric Jerry has used to so articulately defend his

show. Freedom of Speech. The weak and the powerless versus the wealthy and the powerful. The educated versus the uneducated.

"Welcome to America," Jerry told a reporter, "here everybody gets a chance to have their say. I've had Nazis on my show, and they killed a large portion of my family in The Holocaust. But in this country, even someone as vile as a racist is allowed to talk." To another reporter he said, "This format is *supposed* to be outrageous. Not for one second do I believe that the average American is like this. But it's what viewers want."

It's a repetitive theme Springer has cunningly chosen to deflect criticism as, during the last two years the show's subject matter has fallen to new lows amid escalating slugfests, all of which have taken the show to amazing new heights in ratings and viewership. And it's worked. God Bless America!

The one comment no one will ever hear from Jerry, however, is that he is proud of the show bearing his name. A man who prides himself on his honesty and integrity, Springer perpetually and gracefully dodges *that* bullet by focusing instead on the *success* of the show. "Are you proud of the show?" he was asked not long ago. "Sure," he responded. "I'm proud that I've got the success. Is it a show I would watch? No, no. I have no interest. I watch sports and news. I'm hired to be a ringleader of the circus. I'm proud that I do a good job of that. I'm still a Democrat. I'm still liberal. I think the people who watch my show are the ones who voted for me. William Bennett never voted for me. . . ."

Responding to Bennett's anti-trash campaign, Joshua Gamson, a Yale University sociologist, pointed out a short while ago that programs like the Springer show at least allow groups excluded from mainstream society,

such as homosexuals, an opportunity to speak. Behind
Bennett's campaign, he found "the imposition of a particular morality and the desire to shut some people up
and keep them invisible."

However, most media critics disagreed. Howard
Kurtz, *Washington Post* media reporter and author of *Hot
Air*, a new book on talk show culture, was among them.
Kurtz found the supposed benefits proposed by Gamson to be overstated. "The parade of freaks and victims
on these programs," penned Kurtz, "defines deviancy
down in a way that makes bizarre and pathetic behavior
seem almost commonplace."

In the wake of the Jenny Jones controversy and the
increasing outcry about the content of TV talk shows,
the Kaiser Family Foundation, a private organization
that studies health care issues, commissioned a study to
analyze the content of television's top-rated gabfests.
An analysis of 200 videotapes and transcripts of daytime
talk shows was subsequently conducted by Michigan
State University researchers.

What the researchers discovered, along with the fact
that the show's hosts and guests talk mainly about family,
personal relationships, and sex, was that Sally Jessy made
her guests cry, Jerry Springer "outed" his guests, and
Geraldo brought out criminal files. In one way or another, America's talk show hosts were then scoring an
average of sixteen "ambush disclosures" an hour on
their guests, all of whom had little or no control over
the surprise.

"The level of personal disclosures is a trend," said a
Kaiser Foundation spokesman. "In early talk shows
something racy might have been Phil Donahue taking
belly dancing lessons. Now it's all disclosures, particularly about sexual activities.

The study found that the most common disclosures per hour were five of a sexual nature, including one about sexual orientation, four about a personal problem, such as drug addiction, three about abuse, two about an embarrassing situation, and two about a criminal activity. The Kaiser study also discovered that forty-two percent of the disclosures were made by the guests, thirty percent came from other guests and twenty-eight percent were offered by the show hosts.

Interestingly, the 1995 study revealed that Geraldo Rivera had the most criminal disclosures, running seven per hour, but that Jenny Jones revealed more sex secrets, averaging six an hour. Jerry Springer, then in third place for "ambushes," disclosed more sexual orientation surprises, with three revelations per show. Sally Jessy Raphael, focusing on abuse stories at a rate of six per hour, made more guests cry than the rest of her competitors combined. Oprah Winfrey and Phil Donahue, the study concluded, were least likely to disclose "surprise" information, and they also used more experts on their shows.

Several months later, appearing at the National Association of Television Program Executives in Las Vegas, Geraldo, whose talk show of the 1980's had set the stage for the current crop of sensationalistic shows, vowed his show would also clean up its act. "We're getting rid of the sleaze—it's all history," he said, adding, "frankly I was sick of it," a reference to his infamous on-air confrontations with skinheads and neo-Nazis, one of which left him with a black eye and a broken nose in 1989.

A short while after that Geraldo announced he was actually *cancelling* his *Geraldo* talk show and would be relaunching it as *The Geraldo Rivera Show* complete with a new "Bill of Rights and Responsibilities that would emphasize integrity and honesty and solutions rather than shock, and accentuate the positive." It was a remarkable turnabout for the eight-year-old show that had for so long been so criticized as one of TV's tawdriest.

"I began in recent years to feel very seedy about what I was doing," Geraldo later explained to *TIME* magazine, "and yet I was seduced by the big Hollywood money." At the time skeptics noted that Rivera had made the same commitment three times before, and wondered if this was just another publicity stunt on his part. But the mustachioed talk show host kept his word. "We're not going to go into the cycle where if *you* do hookers on your show, *we'll* do hookers and their daughter hookers," he said shortly after announcing his format change. "You can't win that way. You can't win by constantly trying to lowball."

By the time Geraldo had announced he was dismantling his previously salacious program, Oprah Winfrey had already stepped forward and publicly vowed not to indulge in any negative or demeaning subject matter. "There's no honor; no integrity in it," she said of the tawdry TV talk world that surrounded her. "We need to ask programmers for positive role models for ourselves and our children for television that will strengthen the human spirit," she subsequently told *TV GUIDE*.

There were other murmurs of change from the daytime chat crowd, as well. Ricki Lake, for example, announced she was revising her show and revamping its format. Rolonda Watts, whose show also was produced in Chicago, made a similar pledge just prior to her show entering its fourth and, as it turned out, her final season. Mark Walberg pledged to take the same course, but his new talk show got cancelled before it could be implemented. And Richard Bey, whose raucous, ridiculous talk show could have made even *The Jerry Springer Show* producers blush, toned down the topics on his show to the point where his syndicator, All American

Television, dumped him. His demise also marked the
end of several cottage industries, such as the Internet
on-line *Comedy Magazine's* satirical *Fade to Black Awards,*
a weekly award given to "A famous person who we feel
was placed on this earth for no other reason than to
lower our standards."

At one point in 1996, some media watchers were convinced that the talk show market was so saturated that
all of the programs would suffer a decline in viewers.
"There's been a clear shift," wrote Jack Myers, author
of the influential newsletter *Advertising Insights,* that
year. "Many of the talk shows have cleaned up their act,
some have fallen by the wayside and the new ones coming on the air are following a Federal Communications
Commission (FCC) and advertiser-friendly format."
Among the major advertisers cited by Myers as having
pulled their advertising dollars out of the trashier daytime talk shows in the wake of the Amedure murder
were Procter & Gamble, Bristol-Myers, Unilever, Kraft
General Foods and General Motors, most of whom have
never returned to daytime talk sponsorship. "I don't
think they realized how anti-societal much of the con-
tents of these shows was," Myers had explained. But
that was then.

Another sign of a potential turnaround for the show
is that Universal TV, which syndicates the show, is now
reportedly asking double, sometimes triple, the current
licensing fees TV stations pay to carry the show. According to *The Hollywood Reporter,* one station even agreed
to a 500% increase to *renew* its licensing fee.

What Myers and the other media soothsayers could
not see when they were making their 1996 predictions
was that the demise of competition would only create,
as *TIME* magazine later reported, a "nastiness vacuum."

It was a void into which Jerry Springer would cheerfully step and—to the utter amazement and horror of media watchers everywhere—fill with an ongoing parade of bizarre and twisted human flotsam, such as the tragic saga of Denny Welch.

In September, 1996, Jerry and his crew journeyed to Hamilton, Ohio, population 65,000, to pay a visit to the three-room home of Denny Welch, an 860 pound man confined to his bed by his obesity, and tape two segments of what would turn out to be two of the highest rated shows of the season for Springer. The first segment featured an interview between Springer and Welch. After listening intently to Welch's plea for help in losing weight, the talk show host volunteered to be his angel of mercy. Thus, with the cameras rolling and millions of fascinated viewers watching, Springer had the outside wall of Welch's bedroom cut away, a platform built, and Welch, draped in a sheet, hoisted outside by eight bodybuilders from a nearby gym and transported to the town's nearby Christ Hospital for treatment. It was the first time in more than a year that the obese man had seen the sky.

Apparently, however, the weight loss program failed, because two years later, in March, 1998, the thirty-seven-year-old Welch was again in the news, this time after being arrested on three counts of disseminating harmful material to juveniles. According to police, Welch was found lying in bed, again draped in a sheet. Three boys between the ages of eleven and thirteen were in the room, watching pornographic videos from Welch's extensive collection.

At a pre-trial hearing Welch's attorney claimed Welch had been groggy from medication and had been unaware of the boys watching the sexually explicit videos. In Welch's defense, the attorney pointed out that her client "was not physically capable of putting a videotape in a machine and turning it on. Their parents should have kept them out of the house. He can't physically keep them out."

The trial was subsequently rescheduled for late April while the judge figured out how to get the now 1000 pound man into his courtroom. "It takes ten people to move him," explained Welch's attorney, adding that his client suffered from diabetes and high blood pressure.

Interestingly, the two 1996 appearances by Welch were not his first visits to the Springer show. He had been a guest on several of Springer's early shows when the program was being produced in Cincinnati. During those appearances, however, he was billed as a female impersonator known as Eartha Quake. It was his past history with Springer that led him to call the show in search of help for his weight problem, which he found—temporarily. With Welch's latest problem, however, the Springer show is nowhere to be found. They moved on long ago, uncovering even more obese subjects such as a recent program devoted to the sexual problems of "The 1200 Pound Couple."

Last year, in what is apparently an ongoing search for obesity, Jerry took viewers into the bedroom of a woman who he claimed weighed 1600 pounds. He then journeyed to Daytona Beach to explore another kind of weight problem in a show dedicated to "big breasted strippers." It was a subject which one reviewer decided meant "hideously outsized women with enough silicone in their chests to support Intel's computer-chip manufacturing needs for a year."

No wonder he recently joked "We're in fifty countries now and once they see the show they totally lose interest in trying to take us over!"

In November, 1996, Jonathan Schmitz, the guest who had been "surprised" on *The Jenny Jones Show* and later shot and killed the man who had revealed his secret crush on him, was found guilty of second-degree murder and sentenced to twenty-five to fifty years in prison. A year later, in October, 1997, Jenny Jones appeared on *NBC Dateline* in an interview with Jane Pauley. "We don't do anything differently because we don't feel there was anything to change," Jones said, referring to charges that the show was responsible for Schmitz's actions and Amedure's death. "We do the same kind of show. We check out guests the same way. We haven't changed a thing."

It was a disquieting moment of truth because, despite the media predictions not much *had* truly changed. The one exception was *The Jerry Springer Show.* It had changed, all right, but for the *worse,* not for the better. "I remember when we announced the show in 1991, and I was thinking 'Who are we kidding? We'll be lucky to last thirteen weeks!' Now," Jerry gushed in late 1997, "now we're the only crazy show left. All of the others got cancelled. Virtually no new syndicated shows have made it in recent years, except Rosie!"

And the Springer show owes all of its success to its dizzying daily array of uninhibited guests Jerry so articulately defends, guests who have placed him in absolute wonder by their lack of boundaries. In fact, if the critics are puzzled over the guests' uninhibited revelations, the exceptionally private Springer is even more so. He recently recalled the time a woman came home and found her husband in bed with her aunt, then went on his show to talk about it. "It was bad enough that it happened," he said, a trace of awe in his voice, "but they were all there *talking* about it on national TV! It's hard to see why people do this, but they do."

CHAPTER THIRTEEN

No Blame, No Shame

"No one on the planet is surprised anymore by what talk shows are like. They don't think they're going on Queen for A Day."

Jerry Springer

In the two years following the infamous Scott Amedure shooting more than a dozen talk shows came and went—Charles Perez, Rolonda, Gordon Elliott, Mark Walhberg, Tempest Bledsoe, Danny Bonaduce and Richard Bey, along with a number of forgettable newcomers, all had their shows cancelled. What the media soothsayers *hadn't* seen, however, was just how much the Springer show would flourish with the demise of so many of its competitors.

So successful would the Springer show become in filling the "nastiness vacuum" that by the end of 1997 Jerry would be telling reporters, "Since the flak last spring the show has been on an absolute surge. It's totally out of control. You can make a timeline from that week on, and we've grown literally every week. And it's not just kids watching. You can't get numbers like this with just kids. A year ago, everyone thought it was awful. Now that we've got a great audience, it's suddenly fashionable."

While other talk show hosts were either keeping a low profile or making barely audible murmurs of format changes, *The Jerry Springer Show* headed in the opposite direction, pumping up its daily diet of sensationalism—with programs such as "My Wife Weighs 900 Pounds," "I Was Born Both Male and Female," "On Location: First

Female Chain Gang" and "I'm In Love With a Serial Killer"—and laid the blame for the Amedure murder on the public's attitude towards homosexuality, not on *The Jenny Jones Show*.

"It's pretty hard to blame Jenny Jones for murder," he said. "You may not like the show, but that's not an excuse for someone to go murder someone else simply because they don't like the fact that someone who is gay likes them. That shows how homophobic we are in our society. What I mean is . . . imagine on her show, when the person came out, that it wasn't another guy—but a woman. It was a woman whom he thought was ugly, and two days later he killed that woman because he was embarrassed about her saying she loved him on national TV.

"There is not one person who would be blaming Jenny Jones for that murder," he continued. "Instead everyone would be saying, 'How could this guy kill a woman just because he thought she was ugly!' The fact is, at some level, we still think the guy had a right to be humiliated and therefore was somewhat justified in murdering the other guy. That's why the public blames Jenny. The murder trial blames us as a society. The trial is not just about her."

For months following the murder Springer proudly declared to all who inquired, "We've made no changes to the show. The rules are the same. It has to be outrageous. It has to be interesting and it has to be truthful." He was, he continued, totally unconcerned about anything similar occurring during, or after, an appearance on *his* show because "we do things differently."

"We always tell the guests ahead of time if there is going to be some surprise revealed during the show," he explained. "We give them the parameters. When we do shows on secret crushes we tell them that someone is going to come out and say they love you. We give them twenty possibilities—man, woman, schoolmate, Asian, Black. We go through twenty categories, and only if they agree to all of them do they get to be on the show. So they can't say 'I didn't know,' because they sign off on it. We give them twenty choices of what the surprise is going to be and they have to be okay with all of them. But," he also admitted, "we don't tell which one or ones they will actually be."

"Besides," he continued in another interview, "no one on the planet is surprised anymore by what talk shows are like. They know if they get up (on stage) and say bad things, they're going to be booed. They know they're going to meet someone who's going to take the other point of view. They don't think they're going on 'Queen for a Day.' No one gets on a talk show anymore who doesn't want to be on one. We get 3,000 to 4,000 calls a day on our 800 line from people who are begging to be on."

Richard Dominick, the show's executive producer, supports Springer's "It Can't Happen Here" scenario by also pointing out that everyone who calls the show's 800 number is a guest-wanting-to-happen. They *want* to tell their story—and they want to tell it on nationwide TV. Furthermore, says Dominick, every guest is put through an intensive vetting process before they're allowed on the air. "When a person comes on, he knows it's going to be bad," says Dominick. "But we take on people who are willing to roll the dice and deal with it."

"Talk shows will never be in trouble because of the subject matter," Springer once explained. "The more controversial, the bigger the shows get." Besides, both Springer and Dominick repeatedly point out, all of the guests, as well as members of the audience, are searched for weapons before they're allowed into the studio.

* * *

With more than 3,000 callers dialing the Springer show daily, there's obviously no shortage of high-rollers—and Springer is all too willing to give them an opportunity to bare all on national TV, providing they fit his format by not being *too* normal. Ironically, that's the only thing he claims to reject. "It doesn't belong on our show," he explains. "I can't have someone who says they love their kids and drove them to school today. The whole thing is a spoof—fun. It is not meant to be education. So if someone calls up with a nice, heartwarming story, I'm not saying it doesn't belong on TV. I'm saying it doesn't belong on our show. Normal behavior is the only thing we reject."

A perusal of any week's worth of Jerry Springer shows during the past two years proves to validate Springer's dismissal of the normal and the mundane. There isn't "a nice, heartwarming story" among them, unless you count the following March 12, 1998, extravaganza entitled "Update: Love Against The Odds," which began with Jerry telling the audience:

"We received hundreds of letters and phone calls from viewers wanting to know what had happened to a very courageous guest on our show named Janie," Springer begins. "You see, Janie was born without hands or feet. Remarkably, she is totally self-reliant and even has a one-year-old son. When Janie first appeared on our show, she and her boyfriend Doug, who is also the father of Janie's son, were having some major relationship problems. Viewers were outraged at Doug's harsh words to Janie when they were dating. Doug and Janie haven't seen each other since he left her and their baby four months ago. Now Janie has a new boyfriend and she's here today to give Doug a taste of his own medicine!"

* * *

No wonder that in 1996 Springer had begun demeaning the show, calling his program everything from "a circus" to "a cultural cartoon." No wonder that by 1997 he had begun mocking his guests—and sometimes members of his audience—telling them "Go to your room!" as a stern parent would speak to a small child who was either dimwitted or misbehaving. No wonder he feels compelled to *defend* what some would call *the indefensible* by utilizing everything from the inarguable rights of the First Amendment to the arguable suggestion that "If it exists in the world and people want to see it, put it on."

It's precisely this kind of reasoning that is of great concern to Springer's growing legion of critics, and they are many. Where, they ask, is this penchant for the freakish and the bizarre going to ultimately lead? How much more sleazy and outrageous can daytime talk shows become before the public tires of this kind of sensationalism? And then what? Will General Electric soon be sponsoring live telecasts of Florida's "Old Sparky" in electrocuting action? Will Gillette be underwriting live remote telecasts of beheadings from the Middle East?

"People ask me 'Why do you do this wild show?' " Richard Dominick said not long ago. "The answer is 'Because you watch it!' "

Meanwhile, Jerry was telling interviewers "I don't care about my public reputation. If the people who know me know I'm a good person, that's what matters."

CHAPTER FOURTEEN

King of the (Trash) Heap

"Stacy says that even though she cares for her boyfriend, she refuses to give up her career as a stripper. But she may have gone too far when she tells him the whole truth. She's also a call girl and has a lesbian lover, too!"

The Jerry Springer Show

With more than fourteen solid months of sensationalistic daily talk trash behind him, 1997 proved to be a winning year for Jerry. He'd become the uncontested king of the daily talk trash heap and, as such, there was a lot of buzzing going on around him. *PEOPLE* magazine reported the Springer show could count such celebrities as Madonna, Roseanne, and Cher among its more than six million daily viewers and the Nielsen ratings reported that the show's national ratings had increased more than 70%, placing the show in a solid second place behind the Oprah Winfrey show.

Despite the jabs and jeers reported almost daily in the media, however, Jerry was excited, delighted, and amazed by the show's success. He was no longer worried about the competition. "You can't worry about other shows. There's always going to be someone else out there," he told an interviewer. "In every city there are a hundred channels, and there are twenty-four hours in a day. So there is always going to be someone else who is working just as hard or harder to be entertaining. So I just try to make sure we put on the best show we can."

Any trepidation he'd experienced during the first months of Dominick's tabloid-inspired transformation had been totally tossed to the winds. There was no doubt in his mind that the decision to take the low road had led him to high ratings and enormous fame. "I think I was an excellent mayor and lawyer and news anchor and all that," Jerry Springer told a reporter in early 1997, "but this is a wild and crazy show. How I got to do this I'm not particularly sure, but it's a lot of fun. It's gotten wild! I'm the ringleader of a circus now. . . ."

Never mind the jokes, the name-calling, the public outcry, the mounting criticism. He'd experienced all of that, and more, in Cincinnati. Yet, he'd not only survived the prostitution scandal there, he'd flourished. So, with that in mind, Springer decided to handle the subject of his increasingly controversial talk show in the same offhanded, glib manner he had used so adroitly to fend off his detractors in Cincinnati: with humor, honesty and philosophical hubris. It had worked before, he reasoned, and it would work again. For if Jerry Springer has one true talent it is his ability to be at home in a variety of situations with a variety of people—to be part of the flow and yet, somehow, above, beyond, or beside it.

Thus began Jerry's campaign to defend his talk show yet separate himself from the stench emanating from the stage of his Chicago studio. So far he's been fairly successful in remaining aloof from the guests, the melees, and the critic's barbs by offering his own assessments of his show. But if you listen closely to Springer's rhetoric, you begin to realize it's focused more on the "success" of the show than on the show's violence and content.

"It's a cultural cartoon, a purely voluntary show, fun, silly, outrageous," Springer has begun repeatedly telling interviewers. "This is not a show that has any worth other than one hour of escapist entertainment." He echoed this assessment to another dubious reporter, explaining, "This is entertainment. This does not determine what kind of people kids will grow up to be. If we can't have antisocial behavior on TV, then you'll have to do away with local news." And to another scribe he confessed, "Our show is more of a circus than a real confessionary (sic). You know, our show is pure entertainment. I don't know that people come on our show anymore to make confessions. I mean there may be a few, but no one comes to our show for serious counseling. For the moment they're angry, but it's not life and death issues. It's who is dating whom. Compared with the real problems in the world, it's trivial."

While Jerry was busy out front regaling the media and anyone else who was interested with his version, his vision, of *The Jerry Springer Show,* Richard Dominick and his merry band of purveyors of poor taste were diligently working behind the scenes, continuing to pump up the decibels of extreme behavior with an amazing list of show titles, such as "Klanfrontation," "I Want Your Man," "Stop Stalking My Man" and "Surprise! I have Two Lovers!"

The latter Springer Show epic showcased several secret sexual affairs, including the one Jenny was having with Gary, the brother of her boyfriend, Jason. Naturally, as the Springer show producers had hoped, Jason was very, very displeased to learn of Jenny's infidelity. In fact, the minute the brother appeared on stage the two bulky siblings clashed with the force of two water buffalo. But not before the camera cut away for a close-up of Jerry—a stunned, dare we suggest well-studied expression of horror on his pale face—watching Jason topple Gary to the green-carpeted floor. Not a word

had been spoken, and when they were the brotherly
exchange went something like this:

"*Bleep*. He's the only person that you have ever *bleep*.
You been there for her? What the *bleep*. What for, you
bleep. What? *Bleep*. Are you *bleep* me, you *bleep*, *bleep* or
what? You *bleep*, *bleep*, *bleep* . . ."

"Everything else on TV is scripted, edited, sanitized,"
says Springer. "The attraction of this show is that it's
raw. You've got regular people out there and how they
really react. If you suddenly put constraints on them,
well, then we've got what everything else on television
is showing."

Springer even has a rationale for his frequent visits
from the Ku Klux Klan. "Well, I don't tolerate them,"
he explains. "I just tolerate the right of anyone in our
country to express their point of view. I may hate what
they say, but they have the right to say it. And *WE* have
the right in the audience to disagree with them. It was
like when I was a reporter, I often interviewed murder-
ers, people on death row. Just because you interview
people, or permit them to be before the camera, does
not mean that you endorse them. Otherwise every anchor in America would be in jail. They are showing a
slice of the world. The problem with news is that it
shows a very negative view of the world. And they pro-
fess to show us an accurate picture. We *NEVER* maintain
on our show that this is the way most people are, but
news suggests that what they show *IS* how the world is."

Richard Dominick . . . generally regarded as the
brains behind the show's winning formula, couldn't
agree more. "You're seeing real people and real emo-
tion which you don't normally see on television," he
explains. "The studio audience boos the bad guy, and
it becomes a morality play done every day. It doesn't
glamorize everything. It shows you what it is."

As for those critics who bemoan the violence and

sleaze emanating from his show and fear for the minds and souls of viewers young and old, Springer has the perfect answer: "They (the viewers) watch shootings and robberies and rapes. You see promiscuity and infidelity on every soap opera, every prime time show, every comedy, every news program," he says, "and no one ever comes on any of these shows and says, 'That's not appropriate.'

"Our show," he continues, echoing Dominick, "is about the only one where the bad guys actually get booed. None of this misbehavior is made to look attractive. The kids in the audience get it right. They cheer the good guys and boo the bad ones. It's about the only thing on television that gives some kind of a lesson."

And that, say Dominick and Springer, is the reason that the program is not harmful to young viewers—the latchkey kids who watch the show without adult supervision because their parents are away at work with no control over the viewing habits of their offspring. "It shows dysfunctional behavior, but it shows what is appropriate and what is inappropriate," says Springer. "No one of any age is going to say, 'Gee, they're making that look attractive.'"

There have been times when even Springer has felt a twinge of embarrassment, however. Once was the time when he featured a group of adults who practiced a diaper fetish. "Afterward," he told a writer, "I wondered why we did that."

After six seasons of hearing and watching the twice-daily parade of dysfunction, confessions, and on air fights pass by, Springer readily confessed "nothing surprises me anymore." However, there was one intriguing exception. He acknowledged that "People continue to want to talk about their private lives on television surprises me. What they say doesn't—I know all kinds of things go on in the world, I'm not naive. But if it were me, I wouldn't want to talk about it." And that's one of the most interesting facets of Jerry Springer. Despite all of his grand talk, his let-it-all-hang-out-there philosophy, his high profile, apparent openness, and seemingly genuine warmth, Jerry Springer has always been and no doubt always will be an extremely private person.

"I'm not interested in people knowing the details of my life," he told a *TV GUIDE* writer earlier this year, after politely but firmly declining to discuss any portion of his life unassociated with the show. A couple of weeks later, Springer even went so far as to admit to *PEOPLE* magazine that he would "never" be a guest on his own show. "First," he laughingly explained, "I'm a chicken. Second, I wear rented suits. And third, I believe you have your own life and you leave it at home. But that's just my opinion."

The following month Jerry returned to Cincinnati where, with an *Access Hollywood* TV camera crew recording his every word and action, he toured the city in a stretch limousine. He visited City Hall, greeted old friends, posed for photographs and signed autographs for fans, and, like the politician he once was, glad-handed everyone who crossed his path. The whirlwind personal appearance wound up with a speaking engagement at the University of Cincinnati. "I think some talk shows do some good for society," he told the hushed auditorium audience of 800 devoted fans, "but our show shouldn't be called a talk show. There's no talking. They just yell and scream and throw chairs." He laughed.

An hour later, he ended the appearance on an equally jocular note. "I'm absolutely thrilled to call Cincinnati home and I love you all," he gushed. "My greatest wish, particularly for the young people, is that you never appear on my show."

"He was always an anomaly," says John Kiesewetter,

The Cincinnati Enquirer TV critic who has followed Springer's career for more than twenty years.

Anomaly or not, as 1997 ground to a halt Jerry Springer had achieved a new and mind-boggling distinction. Despite the absurdity of his guests and the tawdry content of his show, regardless of his own often ridiculous hyperbole, he had become something akin to a weird culture Pop Icon!

"I think about two or three months ago," he explained to an interviewer, "I just looked at Richard and went, 'Holy s—t! We're now *more* than a television show. We're the subject of someone's cartoon or a reference in a political story in *The Washington Post!*' "

Jerry Springer had also become a cartoon, the butt of unending jokes on every TV show from *Politically Incorrect* to *David Letterman,* who several months ago offered his audience this news flash: "Today a cloned sheep appeared on *The Jerry Springer Show* and was reunited with a woman claiming to be his *sister!*"

CHAPTER FIFTEEN

Battle of the TV Talk Titans

"I'm not a talent, I'm just a schlub that got a show, you know? But Oprah, she's a remarkable talent. . . ."

Jerry Springer

Much to the amazement—and the horror—of his critics, 1997 had been a banner year for Jerry and for his show, literally *and* figuratively speaking. Not only had Jerry risen to the exalted stature of pop culture icon to the MTV crowd as well as the powerless, poor, punching, pushing dysfunctional, his show had achieved something no other talk show had ever even dared hope to accomplish: he had actually beaten Oprah Winfrey in the ratings in several markets.

Jerry Springer had moved up to a solid second place in the national Nielsen November ratings, bumping Rosie O'Donnell into a third place slot. However, the truly awful news to his detractors was that, to their chagrin and dismay, the object of their ongoing derision had knocked Oprah Winfrey, The Diva of Daytime Dish, from her long-held first place ratings perch in the Nielsen ratings in three major American markets—New Orleans, Atlanta and Cleveland! No one had ever come close to Oprah ratings since she, as a young talk show host in Chicago years before, had dethroned talk veteran Phil Donahue and then gone into national syndication.

"SPRINGER TRASHES OPRAH" shouted one news-paper column headline.

"THE LOW ROAD TO HIGH RATINGS" announced a *New York Post* column by Joseph Adalian which began "When it comes to daytime talk, sleaze sells—and nobody does it better than Jerry Springer."

"JERRY SPRINGER ROLLS WITH THE TRASH—AND LOVES IT" penned Jefferson Graham in *USA TODAY*.

Even the venerable *TIME* magazine covered Springer's ratings coup, observing that "the rise of *The Jerry Springer Show* is one of the wonders of the age" and noting that Springer's once mediocre ratings had in the last year improved 183 percent.

Making even a small dent in Winfrey's first place hold on the ratings was an unimaginable feat for a show such as Springer's. The differences between the two shows is an enormous gulf. Even prior to Winfrey's 1995 vow of non-sleaze show subjects, Oprah has never dealt in the kind of sensationalism upon which Springer has built his tabloid kingdom. Moreover, since the year following its national syndication debut in 1986, *The Oprah Winfrey Show* has had the distinction of being the highest-rated talk show in television history, consistently leaving its competitors in the ratings dust. It is seen by more than fifteen to twenty million viewers a day in the U.S. and is syndicated in more than 130 countries. During its twelve consecutive seasons of broadcasting the program has received thirty Emmy Awards, six of which were handed personally to Oprah, who also has been honored with The George Foster Peabody Individual Achievement Award.

The people at Winfrey's production company, Harpo Productions, claimed to be unfazed by the loss. "Oprah's not looking over her shoulder at this year's second-best flavor," Tim Bennett, president of Harpo

Productions, told the press. "Over the last twelve years we've had probably eight different Number Twos. Last year it was Rosie (O'Donnell). The year before it was Ricki (Lake), and two years before that it was Sally (Jessy Raphael). This is just another Number Two."

However, when the next two ratings periods reflected a continued gain by Springer, whose ratings by February 22, 1998, had risen 183 percent, even Oprah, The Queen of Gab, had to admit that Jerry, The King of Trash, had become a force with which to be reckoned. "Yes," she told Bryant Gumbel, during an appearance on his NBC show *Public Eye,* "I'm being beaten by Jerry Springer in Atlanta. Yes, I am," she reiterated in mock sorrow. Listed by *Forbes* magazine as the third highest paid entertainer in the business, with an income of $201 million and an estimated wealth of $550 million, Oprah has little to worry about regarding her future. In fact, in recent years, long before Jerry Springer sprang into ratings view, Winfrey had begun talking about leaving her talk show behind and moving into other areas. It is a move that may well be just around the corner if the astute Winfrey determines that the American public prefers daytime garbage to gourmet discourse.

Not surprisingly, Springer was exuberant about the meteoric climb his show had taken in the ratings. "No one owns up to it," he told a reporter during a phone interview from England, where he was delivering a lecture on his favorite subject, Freedom of Speech, at Oxford University, "but *someone* must be watching the show."

As ever, Richard Dominick echoed those sentiments. "I feel we have a show people like," he said, adding, "critics may not like it, but people like it."

In a press release sent out immediately after the February, 1998, Nielsen ratings had been announced, the Springer publicity department heralded the fact that he had become the first person to topple Winfrey from her exalted perch at the top. However, not everything is always quite as it appears to be—and this may be the case in what has become the ongoing Battle of the Talk Show Titans.

First of all, *The Jerry Springer Show* airs twice daily in twenty-three of the thirty-eight major Nielsen markets, whereas Winfrey's show runs twice daily *only* in Chicago. When you take the double telecasts into account, Springer's ratings drop almost a point, giving Oprah the lead. Secondly, in several markets the Winfrey show is carried on CBS stations and had been preempted due to the network's telecasts of the Winter Olympics from Japan. Thirdly, and perhaps more importantly, Winfrey had spent most of January and February in the backwaters of Amarillo, Texas, defending herself against a $10.3 million slander suit. It had been filed by a coalition of Texas cattle barons who had taken umbrage at remarks about the dangers of Mad Cow Disease and the consumption of beef made by vegetarian Howard Lyman during an April, 1996, appearance on Oprah's show.

The trial had begun in mid-January—only two days after Winfrey had flown in on her private Gulfstream jet accompanied by an entourage including her bodyguard, personal chef, her two pet cocker spaniels and most of her Oprah show staff—and had lasted until late February. During her time in Amarillo, Oprah had spent only three days on the stand; but even then she couldn't escape the looming spectre of Jerry Springer. Under cross-examination by Joe Coyne, the cattlemen's attorney, Oprah was confronted with the fact that Springer had beaten her ratings in New Orleans.

"And you don't like that, do you?" Coyne had thundered.

"Well," Oprah had replied, making no effort to hide her disdain, "Jerry has his show and I have mine."

Throughout her lengthy Texas sojourn Oprah taped her talk show at the Amarillo Little Theater, flying in guests like singer Garth Brooks and actor Patrick Swayze in an effort to keep the show afloat without having to fall back on repeats. "I felt it was important to be here to face this courtroom and the jurors and to defend my name," she told the packed courtroom, adding, "in the end, all you have is your reputation."

Six weeks after she'd arrived in Amarillo—where an estimated 10,000 visitors had shown up to attend an Oprah taping or buy the souvenir T-shirts, buttons, banners, and caps proclaiming Amarillo Loves Oprah (or the flashy caps and T-shirt declaring, The only mad cow in Texas is Oprah)—Winfrey was back in Chicago, picking up the pieces of her life and the reins of her show.

As Oprah had implied under oath in Amarillo, the differences between her show and Jerry Springer's are distinct, and dramatically underscore the evolved—and the *un*evolved—personalities of their hosts in terms of social and moral responsibility and entertainment values. Nothing reflects these opposites than a look at the topics presented by Oprah and Jerry during that heavily contested ratings week of February 16, 1998. Springer was offering viewers a titillating taste of "I'll Never Let You Go," "Sex With My Sister," "When Past Guests Attack," "Home Wreckers Confronted" and "Honey, I'm A Call Girl." And, from Amarillo, Oprah was dishing with celebrities Celine Dion, David Schwimmer, Carroll O'Connor, and Hanson, as well as the cast of *The Wedding*, a miniseries produced by her company.

"Mentioning me in the same breath with Oprah is really unfair to Oprah," Springer once said to an interviewer. "She's the best there is. She's a real talent. I'm not a talent, I'm a *schlub* (a Yiddish expression for nerd, geek, or loser) that got a show, you know? My background and training isn't in television. This is not a particular skill that I have. I'm just lucky enough to have a very popular show; but, Oprah, she's a remarkable talent, and so is Rosie. We just have a show now that is so outrageous, it's captured the public's imagination. That's what it is—it's a momentary blip on the screen. But, you know, twenty years from now they're gonna remember Oprah, they're not gonna remember me."

Momentary blip? Probably. Forgotten? Absolutely not true. Twenty years from now Jerry Springer will still be remembered as the Sultan of Sleaze who forever changed the face of syndicated daytime television talk shows. It is a legacy about as attractive as the content found on his show. Apparently the people back in Cincinnati agree. In 1997 they voted Springer "Worst Talk Show Host" in a poll conducted by *The Cincinnati Enquirer*.

"I think that came out of people who remembered and respected him here," explained John Kiesewetter, the paper's TV critic. "A lot of people feel sad and even a bit hurt to see such a bright, intelligent guy, who was a true leader in the city council here doing such topics as 'Confess, You Liar!' as opposed to the real contributions he once made."

THE CONTROVERSIES

> "There are lots of little murders going on with this show—of the soul, of the sensibility of its viewers. It's gossip without any penalties—none for the viewers, that is, except for a coarsening of their sensibilities."
>
> Leo Braudy, Professor
> University of Southern California

CHAPTER SIXTEEN

The Sour Smell Of Success

"We're not going to show you how to reduce your taxes, you won't learn anything, we won't bring peace to the world, but just admit it—we're entertaining."

Jerry Springer

By mid-February, 1998, Jerry Springer had become the catalyst for controversies, large and small, from a small town down south in Virginia to the motor city up north, Detroit. In between there'd been a major skirmish in Chicago that had landed him on the entertainment pages of most of the country's major newspapers. Everyone, it seemed to Jerry, was mad, not just the people who were punching, gouging, and cursing each other on his show. And the higher his ratings climbed, the angrier people seemed to be getting.

Yes, his name had certainly become a household word. Yes, every important magazine and newspaper had carried stories on him and the show bearing his name. But the adjectives that were being attached to his name were not exactly what Jerry Springer had envisioned when he was standing on the bottom rung of the ladder of success. The nation's television critics were pounding him in print. Several United States Senators were hounding him in Washington. Even revered TV executives, men he admired, were berating him for being a willing participant in what they deemed "A Theater of the Perpetual Scandal."

Yes, by early 1998, the name Jerry Springer had become synonymous with any subject that smelled of tabloid sleaziness, be it local or national, small time or big time. Overnight Jerry Springer had become a character to lampoon in print and cartoons. His name had become a yardstick of measurement for all that was deemed to be bizarre and raunchy, whether it was the revelations of a celebrity scandal or the twisted tale of an unknown citizen. Overnight, Jerry Springer had become a lightning rod for trouble.

For instance, in February, the Detroit City Council's nine member body had drafted a resolution requesting that Springer's program be aired in the morning instead of the afternoon and submitted it to WDIV-TV, the station responsible for bringing the Springer show into the city's living rooms.

"Kids in the city don't need to have it on at four," explained Councilwoman Kay Everett. What the show does, she explained "is really condone violence" and, she added, the show's material could only have a negative impact on children. Thrilled by the ratings it was garnering prior to its 5 P.M. newscast, the station refused to move the show from its controversial afternoon berth.

"The input we get is basically overwhelmingly in favor of keeping the show in its current time slot," said Henry Maldonado, the station's vice-president of programming and promotions. "The show is closer to comedy than public affairs, and to look at a show like Jerry and put any kind of priority of it over some of the issues that do bring cities down is funny at best." Within days, however, a group of outraged parents had picketed the station to protest the afternoon telecast. It didn't change anything, but it made them feel better.

Less than two weeks later Julie Kidwell, the principal of Ghent Elementary School in Norfolk, Virginia, sent a note home asking that parents bar their kids from watching the combative and usually lurid Springer show. The note was written after teachers complained that frequent "Springer style" brawls with fists or chairs had spilled over into the schools classrooms and playgrounds.

"It has come to the attention of the staff that many of our students are watching *The Jerry Springer Show,*" the note began. "While we do not discourage any adult from watching programming of their choice, we do want to voice our concern about the content of this particular show and the negative impact it has had on our children."

"I hate that show," said Leola Brown, a guidance counselor at another Norfolk elementary school. "The influence is very, very strong here," she said, explaining one student had told her she was skipping class to tune in the program.

"I think it's funny because they're yelling and fighting," the twelve-year-old had told her. "I think it's bad, though," Brown said. "Kids act 'Jerry Springer' out in school, pulling their hair. They pretend to fight." The pre-teen had begun watching the program once a week, but gets daily updates during homeroom and lunch periods from young classmates. Her mother began watching the show after hearing the kids talk about it and now can't turn it off. "It might give the kids the wrong idea," the mother admitted. "They might think they can hit someone and assume that's okay. I watch it because I'm amazed by the violence on TV. I want to see how far it's going to go."

Springer remains absolutely unrepentant and unapologetic towards the still growing number of educators and parents who claim his show reflects, and perhaps is even partly responsible for, the moral decay they believe is permeating America today. To those who would believe his program is unhealthy—perhaps even unholy—for the nation's youth, Jerry has a response. "In the twelve hundred shows I've done in the last seven years," Jerry shot back at his detractors, "never once have the kids in the audience ever cheered a racist or a wife beater or a woman who's cheating on her husband. Every single time, the kids in the audience get it right. They understand what is morally acceptable and what isn't."

To another reporter he explained, "Virtually every night, I was covering murders, war, rapes, armed robbery. If I read a story about a murder that took place in my community," he continued, referring to his career as a TV news anchorman in Cincinnati, "that didn't mean that I advocated the practice of murder, did it? Well, my featuring alternate life-styles on my show also doesn't connote that I endorse people to go out and practice that."

Last March (1998) two Democratic senators lent their voices to the growing chorus of Springer foes. Joining William Bennett, former Secretary of Education and author of *The Book of Virtues,* in his quest to rid the nation's airways of "cultural rot," Senators Joe Lieberman (D-Conn.) and Dan Coats (R-Ind.) had authored a joint letter to Education Secretary Richard Riley concerning the Education Department's $8 million a year grants for closed-captioning for the hearing impaired. Supported by tax-payer dollars, these subsidies are intended for news programs, movies, children's programming, and other opportunities for the hearing-impaired to enjoy "enriched educational and cultural experiences."

The senators had learned that *The Jerry Springer Show* had been receiving a closed-captioning subsidy of approximately $65,000 annually, and they wanted to know why. Believing that the Springer show should not be seen, let alone heard, they also wanted Secretary Riley to revoke the grant and review the guidelines on funding.

> *"The Jerry Springer Show is the closest thing to pornography on broadcast television," they wrote. "It regularly features such perverse subject matter as pregnant strippers, teen-age prostitutes, and undertaker sex, and characteristically exploits and revels in the problems of its guests. Short of the window it provides on the depths to which our culture has sunk, we challenge anyone to demonstrate how it may legitimately 'educate' the public."*

Again there was an outcry, this time from the nation's hearing-impaired television watchers. But, unlike the other furors created by the Springer show, in this instance Jerry found he actually had supporters on his side of the still pending issue that has caused a flurry of action by some powerful organizations.

Jerry Thixton, the president of the Indiana Association of the Deaf, defended deaf people's rights to tune in and watch the antics. "It," he said, referring to the Riley letter, "implies we would be considered second-class citizens. I hope that we will not turn the clock back." The National Association of the Deaf also entered the fray, initiating a letter-writing campaign in defense of the show's closed-captions. And deaf people across the land began fighting for their right to "hear" the show. "A lot of people are sending letters," said Brenda Arnold, a case manager for Deaf Community Services in Indianapolis. "If they want to remove that captioning, they should take away the voice part, too. I enjoy the show."

"We're not going to show you how to reduce your taxes, you won't learn anything, we won't bring peace to the world, but just admit it—we're entertaining," Springer countered to his critics.

The upset concerning the content of Springer's daily theater of the bizarre, however, is not confined only to educators, parents, and government officials. Even broadcast executives are beginning to cringe when confronted with the name Jerry Springer. Grant Tinker, the former husband of Mary Tyler Moore and creator of MTM Productions, as well as past president of NBC-TV, is an honored, well-respected member of the television industry. So, when he lashed out at Springer during a convention of program executives last year, it made an impact on both the attendees and the media.

"I think Springer is the worst I've seen of the breed. This pandering, this selling out to these least common denominator tastes, I think is deplorable. They just feed on human misery, or create it, as the case may be. It sounds old-fashioned and priggish, but someone has to say it," Tinker later said, adding he blames the messenger, not the audience that enjoys the message. "You can't take them all to task," he admitted. "You've got to go to the source and say, 'Jerry Springer, you're a disgrace. Don't do that anymore.' If he wasn't giving it to them," Tinker said, "it wouldn't be there for them to watch. Sometimes you've got to go right to the head of the snake and cut it off."

Unruffled by Tinker's well-publicized blast at him, Springer countered, "Look, I may very well enjoy watching Grant Tinker's stuff a lot more than mine," he responded. "That's my personal taste. But this show isn't about my personal taste. That would be arrogant. The stations aren't giving me an hour each day to put on what Jerry Springer likes. If I did my show every day, it'd be Yogi Berra and politics. That's what I like in life. But I was hired to do a show about outrageousness. That's my job. So I have to, every day, put on something that's outrageous. My show fails if, one day, I put on normal behavior."

Although Tinker has been just one of the few industry bigwigs to speak out publicly against *The Jerry Springer Show*, there are many other people within the television industry who feel the same way about the show's content. Even people within the talk show area itself have become somewhat dismayed and disgusted by the Springer show and the bad name they believe it is giving the genre. "Jerry Springer is an irresponsible program that doesn't worry about what happens afterward," claims Stuart Krasnow, a former producer for *The Ricki Lake Show*. "I'd hate to see something terrible happen but . . . when the rules start going away, when you push the envelope for too long, something happens."

Yet the torrential downpour of criticism flows over Springer like water off a duck's back. "Ask the viewers," Springer says. "They obviously think we're an entertaining show. We're not going to show you how to reduce your taxes, you won't learn anything, we won't bring peace to the world, but just admit—we're entertaining."

In the manner of the lawyer he once was, Springer has become a master of First Amendment rhetoric, claiming his program is honest, his program is responsible, his program defends freedom of speech, and his program gives a voice to the voiceless. It is an attorney's way of defending the indefensible. Even more interesting, though, is that Springer has found a way to simultaneously position himself on *both* sides of the talk show issue—defending free speech while at the same time demeaning the show, calling it "a circus, a cultural cartoon." It's a curious defense, a kind of double speak designed to lend a certain substance to a show he admittedly thinks is "silly."

"I'm the ringleader of this circus, you know. So I just don't take it that seriously. Maybe that's why I sleep well. We'll let anyone on the show as long as their story is outrageous. We'll bleep out the foul language, but we won't censor their ideas or positions even though we may find them distasteful. This is just a silly show about outrageousness."

CHAPTER SEVENTEEN

The Critics Rave

"On Jerry Springer gargantuan boobs apply not only to the female anatomy but also to Springer's guests."

Howard Rosenberg
Los Angeles Times

In the minds and columns of the nation's television pundits, the Jerry versus Oprah ratings war has become something akin to a raging battle in which the forces of good and evil are pitted against each other in a daily fight for the very souls of television viewers everywhere. By Spring, 1998, Springer had become more than simply a joke, "a cultural cartoon." He had become a merchant of sleaze, a glib exploiter of the weak and the stupid for his own fame and fortune.

With the ratings soaring, along with the show's number of viewers, the host and the staff of the Springer show could not have cared less about newspaper cartoons lampooning the show. Instead they found it amusing, often tacking the jokes to the wall of the production office, such as the cartoon which read: "Talk shows: Do they distort reality? We'll ask these three morbidly sweaty serial killers with overbites on the next Springer."

"Look, we're a totally different show than Oprah," Jerry continued reminding his critics. "As I've said before, our show is not going to save humanity—or destroy it. I still Believe Oprah is the best. And I don't think I can beat Oprah in terms of national popularity. I think we're about as high as we can get."

Nevertheless, if his detractors had taken him seriously in the past, by the beginning of 1998 they had been forced to take Jerry Springer and his self-proclaimed circus of outrage *very* seriously. And they did, dubbing him The King of Sleaze and the show everything from "the dark side of *The Beverly Hillbillies*" to "a three-ring circus of daytime sleaze."

"On Jerry Springer, gargantuan boobs apply not only to the female anatomy but also to Springer's guests," wrote Howard Rosenberg, TV critic for the *Los Angeles Times*.

"On Jerry Springer," penned another scribe, "pre-operative transsexuals mingle with postoperative lobotomies, hotheads with empty heads, human cabbages with potatoes."

"Springer is the flavor of the month—and daytime TV viewers are sampling his naughty treats before they grow stale," proffered an East Coast critic in a dubious moment of optimism.

"I don't think Jerry Springer goes home and pulls wings off flies," Jeff Greenfield, a respected author and ABC media commentator, confided to a reporter, "but that's exactly what he does on the show."

Another newspaper television reviewer even pondered in print where it was all going to end. He finally reached the conclusion, as he wrote, that journalistic limits would not be reached until programs such as Springer's began doing surprise on-air death notifications—"Actually, we're not interested in your lemon cake recipe, Mrs. Smythe, you're here because—Surprise!—your husband is dead!"

"The Jerry Springer Show performs a public service, providing the only chance trailer-trash get to be TV stars," penned yet another critic.

Even Rosie O'Donnell, herself a talk show host, had an opinion about the Springer show, insights she shared during an interview with former daytime talk show host Merv Griffin. Rosie compared the Springer show to televised wrestling. Merv concurred, nodding his head, as the comedienne told her audience, "Viewers know it's fake, but they watch it . . . and somehow they feel a little better about their lives, that they are not as pathetic as the people on Jerry Springer."

"Springer is the king of tabloid TV," wrote a London critic after the Springer parade had made its way to the airwaves of Great Britain via satellite. "Dysfunctional families don't need therapy, they need publicity. And they need the opportunity for a good fist fight in front of millions of television viewers."

"After some early promise, Springer has devolved into talk TV's leading *sleazemeister*, a leerer without a cause," wrote a TV critic, citing shows such as "I Strip with My Family," "Honey, Please Don't Join the Klan," "Newlyweds on the Verge of Divorce," "The Woman I Love is a Man" and "I'm Raising My Daughters to Hate Men," a show about mothers encouraging their daughters to become lesbians, as proof of Springer's decline.

"The Springer show isn't illegal—it's just in poor taste," a reviewer for the *New York Post* ultimately decided.

"That shameless phony Sally Jessy has always presented herself as Mother Teresa while exploiting for profit the pathetically gnarled lumps she professes to care so deeply for. In contrast, Springer proudly wears sleaze and slime like a chest full of medals," wrote Howard Rosenberg, television critic of the *Los Angeles Times* in a scathing exploration of the appeal of the show. "He's blatant about doing this for laughs, cheerfully sacrificing his guests on the altar of lowbrow entertainment, then casting them aside like one of weepy Sally Jessy's tissues."

"The sad thing about all the raunchiness is that it seems designed only to shock us into not changing the channel," offered Terence Mahon, professor of culture and communications at New York University.

Not everyone, of course, has been stridently assailing Jerry and his show. He does have one supporter—and a big name celebrity as well. Roseanne who, beginning in September, 1998, will take to the airways on 150 stations with her own daily talk show, is an ardent Springer fan. "I just love Jerry Springer," she told a 1997 convention of television executives, adding that she was firmly convinced the people appearing on the Springer show were real, not staged. "I know," she explained, "because after ten years in Hollywood I know there are no writers smart enough to make that stuff up."

Although Roseanne's show is being produced and distributed by King World, the same company responsible for distributing *Oprah, Geraldo,* and two TV tabloid magazine shows—*American Journal* and *Inside Edition*—the comedienne promised that *her* show would not delve into sensational topics.

Through it all, and despite it all, however, both Springer and his show have continued to rise—the show in the ratings, the host to the defense. "It's difficult to upset the equilibrium of a man who has no shame," wrote an interviewer after having spent several hours listening to Springer's philosophy on why his show is not what everyone is calling it. "This is entertainment, pure and simple," Springer had told him. "It has to be entertaining because we are in show business. I make no apologies for the show. Heck, I'm not mayor of Cincinnati anymore. I don't have to conform to that mindset.

"If I have three professors sitting there debating the

psychological effects of this or that, people turn me off," Springer had explained, adding, "my sense of morality in doing the show is predicated on the stance I take on an issue."

It's this kind of repetitive, philosophical gibberish that has made his former constituents in Cincinnati question just who is Jerry Springer. He has, in their minds, turned out not to be the man they thought he once was. Thus, last year, the city's readers expressed their disgust with his on air antics by voting him the "Worst TV host" in a poll taken by *The Cincinnati Enquirer.*

Even several of the nation's most powerful advertisers have shown their displeasure with *The Jerry Springer Show.* Sponsors such as Sears, Unilever and Procter & Gamble cancelled their advertising contracts with seven "objectionable" talk shows following the Scott Amedure murder in 1995; and, although they have returned to several of the toned down gabfests they have not journeyed back to *The Jerry Springer Show.* It is a fact that the show's executives would prefer not be known. "Nothing has changed," a spokesperson for Procter & Gamble recently confirmed. "The content of the Springer program is not consistent with the guidelines we use to evaluate programs we think are a suitable environment for our brands." However, the same may not necessarily be true for other sponsors.

The world of television has changed drastically in the last two years for *The Jerry Springer Show,* which has seen its home audience climb from three million to eleven million viewers this year. This astonishing gain has not gone unnoticed by mainstream advertisers, who because of the ratings may not be so adverse to associating themselves with transvestites, the fights, and the sexual situations that abound on the show. "The wall of resistance is breaking down," an industry executive acknowledged in a recent *ADWEEK* article.

"Three or four months ago there was a lot of advertiser resistance to Jerry," said Don Corsini, general manager of KCAL, an independent Los Angeles television station which carries the Springer show twice daily. "There still is some, but you just can't ignore the success and the demographics. It's really turning around. Jerry's like a cult hero and, bizarre as it seems, there are a lot of CEO types who are closet Jerry Springer viewers."

Besides, the cost of advertising on the Springer show is far less than that of its competitors. Compared to Rosie O'Donnell's thirty second rate ($60,000) and Oprah Winfrey's ($85,000), advertising on Springer for $30,000 is an absolute half-priced bargain. But not a bargain apparently for the stations carrying the program. According to a recent *Hollywood Reporter* article, Universal TV, which syndicates the show, is now asking double, sometimes triple, the current license fees TV stations pay to carry the show; and, in one instance even managed to get a station to agree to a 500 percent increase in the fees.

At one point in early 1998, Springer told an interviewer he thought people were angry at the success of his show, and that their anger could be traced to an elitist attitude. "Television historically—there's this tremendous pressure to only reflect white, upper middle-class values in our society, and anything that has been different historically breaking in to capture the attention of the camera has met resistance," he explained. "In the beginning you couldn't find blacks on television. And today it's almost—it's not so much the show, they don't like the people. You know, it's like 'How did *those* people get on television?' You hear so much of that. You always hear the derogatory comment about 'trailer park trash,' you know? I mean, it's *so* elitist."

To some psychologists and sociologists, however, *elitism* has absolutely nothing to do with either *The Jerry Springer Show* or its impact upon America, a nation they claim is now in its Golden Age of Gross—and it's not *gross* income or tonnage they're talking about. "You are what you consume," says Robert Knight, director of cultural studies for the ultraconservative Family Research Council in Washington. "And right now Americans are being fed a steady diet of vulgarity. Once a culture starts coarsening, there really is no end in sight."

Robert J. Thompson, professor at Syracuse University's Center for The Study of Popular Television, echoes Knight's comments. "Any respectable declining great civilization is always accompanied by these perverse circus-like activities," he points out.

And, of course, that's exactly what *The Jerry Springer Show* has become. By Springer's own admission, "It's a circus—just a silly show about outrageousness." As the show has begun depending more and more upon violence and the bizarre to woo viewers into the center ring, however, psychologists have begun expressing greater concern about the Springer show, its impact upon viewers and, more importantly, the impact upon its guests.

"There are lots of little murders going on with this show—of the soul, of the sensibility of its viewers," claims Leo Braudy, a professor and specialist on mass media and popular culture at the University of Southern California. "It's gossip without any penalties—none for the viewers, that is, except for a coarsening of their sensibilities."

Braudy's main concern, however, is the emotional well-being of the Springer show guests. "The main reason people appear on these shows is they're thinking that this will solve the problem," he explains, adding, "and, of course, it doesn't. Sometimes it makes their problems worse because they're exposed and a lot of volatile emotions are released."

Jeanne Heaton, an Ohio University psychologist, agrees. "Some people think it's great to humiliate people, see their misfortune, and laugh at it," says Heaton, who has written *Tuning in Trouble,* a book exploring the effects of trashy talk shows on mental health. "But it hardens you to real problems that people suffer. Our research indicates that what audiences like are the fights and the really outrageous behavior," she says of the Springer show. And it's a natural reaction. "Think about it. If you're walking along the street and you saw a fight breaking out, you'd stop to look. People are drawn to the commotion."

Both Braudy and Heaton believe that talk show producers are exhibiting a reckless disregard for the emotional fragility of troubled people. "It doesn't take much," Heaton points out, "if you take volatile people and reward them for their violent outrageous behavior, to flip them over the edge."

Jerry Springer and his producer, Richard Dominick, of course, couldn't disagree more. Even after the most violent slugfests on his shows, Springer points out, "Everyone gets together in the studio's Green Room and says, 'Can we have pictures?' It's like most people," he says. "They blow off steam, and life goes on." But does it? Or, as in the case of Jonathan Schmitz and Scott Amedure, will it ultimately lead to violence? When it comes to the future of shows like *The Jerry Springer Show* there appear to be as many opinions as there are people.

"The fact is, television is a business, and it's always going to go for the lowest common denominator to grab an audience," explains Lauryn Axelrod, the author of *TV-Proof Your Kids,* a parent's guide to television. "Will we see the F-word on network television?" she responds. "I've no doubt about it. Will we see graphic sex or public executions on television? I'm sure. There's nowhere else to go but down. After all," she points out, "it is called *broad*-casting, isn't it? Television," she adds, "can be disgustingly awful, and it can be wonderful and enlightening. And somewhere in the middle is *Gilligan's Island.*"

Axelrod believes that the answer to programs like *The Jerry Springer Show* is not censorship but education, whereby viewers become "educated consumers of culture, not merely passive swillers of the vilest pop culture *dreck.*"

And *dreck* appears to be an increasing specialty of the Springer show in its search for new, exotic realms of absurdity and its ongoing campaign to retain its ratings place in television history. Take, for example, the program featuring a "naked human bowling ball" on the same show as a stripper named Brandy whose sole claim to fame was satisfying men possessing a sexual fetish for consuming breast milk.

"Basically," Brandy explained to the engrossed studio audience, "I spray it into a glass and people, uh, drink it."

Jerry was stunned. "Isn't that downright perverted?" he asked.

Brandy didn't appear to think so.

"Isn't that kind of sacred?" Jerry insisted, determined to retrieve some hint of philosophy from the woman. It was not to be.

"Oh, I have more than enough to spare," Brandy replied, adding, "it *is* nutritional."

No wonder that after the show aired Jerry once again was telling the media that nothing shocked him. "I don't know if that's just because of the show. I think it's pretty hard for those of us who are my age or older, you've seen so much already in the world—a presidential assassination, a shuttle explosion, the wall in Berlin come down. I don't know if I can be shocked by anything. We've seen it all. It's not the subjects that amaze me. It's the fact that people are willing to share their secrets."

Most of the time Springer is barely able to keep a straight face. On more recent shows he hasn't even attempted to try. For instance on a March, 1998, show which featured two women fighting over the same man, a skinny little nerd with the face of a mouse and the hair of Albert Einstein, Springer actually laughed when the object of their affection strode out on stage. "This is it?" he said. "This is what you're fighting over?" The audience howled.

"No stronger thread bonds the disparate social and economic classes of America today than the desire to be on television—a point underscored daily by afternoon TV shows where seemingly normal people tell deeply humiliating stories about themselves because they sense, correctly, this is what it takes to get on," wrote critic-at-large David Hinckley in a 1997 column published in the *New York Post*.

"People happily married for fifty years may get a 'Hello' from Willard Scott," added Hinckley. "People married twelve times who sleep with their sisters get their own Jerry Springer episode."

As for the violence continually exhibited on the show, one astute observer offered this summation: "Even when they deserve what's coming," he wrote of the show's guests, "it all starts feeling like a mean schoolyard taunt."

CHAPTER EIGHTEEN

Fifteen Minutes of Fame

"Most people's deepest fear is anonymity. That no one notices or cares. Being on TV says you exist."

Dr. Joy Brown, psychologist

Appearing on television seems to be becoming a national obsession. Everyone—from grocery clerks to garbage collectors, housewives to hookers—is suddenly in search of his fifteen minutes of fame. Or, in the case of *The Jerry Springer Show,* fifteen minutes of *shame.* Apparently it's an easy quest to fulfill. The Springer show's 800 number is ringing off the wall these days with calls from viewers responding to the show's repeated on-air quest during commercial breaks for the bizarre and the ridiculous.

"Are you married or dating a man who has another woman pregnant with his child right now? If so, call us and tell us about it."

"Do you have an unusual life-style that your family disapproves of, and they want to disown you? If so, call us and tell us about it."

"We get a lot of people who call and tell us, 'I've got three eyes' or 'I'm sleeping with my pet goat,' " said Annette Grundy, a senior producer. "People think that s--- is funny." Apparently, so does the Springer show staff. After all, the show did produce a segment featuring a woman who seriously believed she'd been born on Venus.

With so many people clamoring for their moment of

shame, the show rarely pays appearance fees for guests.
But they do get free airfare to Chicago, free meals, a
hotel stay, even a limousine ride. "Yes there are consequences of being on a talk show," a producer acknowledged. "But our guests can say yes or they can say no.
If they say yes, the rest is on them. Don't you dare try
to blame a talk show for your homicide." Besides, the
program occasionally offers post-show counseling to
any guests they deem needing it after their onstage
emotional experience. Few guests accept the offer.
"We've done maybe three in the course of a year," recalled Dominick.

It used to be that only select members of society
sought fame via the bright lights of Broadway, the big
screens of movie houses, or the small screens so promi-
nently placed in the nation's living rooms. Now everyone has the chance to be a television star, if only for a
brief, fleeting moment.

"You don't even have to do anything on television,"
says Dr. Joy Browne, a psychologist and host of a nationally syndicated radio show. "You just have to be
there. It validates your life. Most people's deepest fear
is anonymity. That no one notices or cares. Being on
TV says you exist. You matter. Your life matters." And
that means any life, from trailer park to Park Avenue.

Barbara Tucker, a thirty-six-year-old Alabama woman,
is a case in point. She fully understands the appeal of
being on television. She's been on three different talk
shows to berate her "bitch" of a sister-in-law. She regrets
the time she went on the Springer show, however. "We
shouldn't have gone on. I got upset on that show," she
says. "My mother didn't speak to my brother for a long
time."

But even though she's drawn a line through Jerry's
show, she still wants to do more. "I like to get out there
and priss," she explains.

Michelle Van Buren, a thirty-one-year-old Missouri woman who appeared on *Geraldo* to discuss men who lie and cheat, is aware that the daytime talk shows "exploit people." But, she says, she doesn't care. "I've always been a homebody," she explains. "I never wanted to talk. But it's like I broke out of my shell. I just love it. And," she exulted, "they put on great makeup!"

Not everyone, of course, is appearing on the talk shows just for the fun of it. Some of the guests, like the white supremacists and the neo-Nazis, have an obvious political agenda. And, unlike Barbara Tucker and Michelle Van Buren, not all guests exit *The Jerry Springer Show* feeling their lives have been enhanced by the experience. This was the case in October, 1996, when two groups of people were invited to fly to Chicago, all expenses paid, and discuss the more intimate details of their respective lives on a segment titled "I'm Jealous of My Gay Friend." In the end three of the participants were angered enough to discuss their misadventures on the show with the media.

The show featured two groups of friends—one from California in which a married woman thought her husband was spending too much time with a gay neighbor, and one from North Carolina in which a straight woman thought she'd be complaining about a gay friend acting haughty. As it turned out, however, to her surprise she ended up having to defend herself against charges from her gay friend that she was making sexual overtures to him and his friends.

Within days of having appeared on the Springer show, several of the guests contacted a reporter for the *Chicago Tribune* and charged that the Springer show experience had included everything from the producers urging them to display anger, even get physical, to telecasting nasty onscreen captions during the segment. Two of the women guests also accused the show's producers of trying to coax them into wearing skimpy or stereotypical clothing. Moreover, they claimed the producers had promised perks to lure them to Chicago and then had not delivered some of them. One of the guests also believed that at least one audience member who asked questions on camera during the taping had been planted in the crowd and was in truth affiliated with the show.

Not surprisingly, the show vehemently denied each and every charge made by the disenchanted guests. Brenda You, the producer who put the show together, denied the accusations, saying if they were true it would be a violation of show policy. "Everything we promised we did. There were no mean little statements written under their names. There was no secret subject change or title change. There was no encouragement of a fight, and there was no fight. They came on because they wanted to be on national TV and now they're in the newspaper because they want to be in the press," You claimed. "This was kind of a light show," she added. "I'm surprised they'd even be upset about it."

However, You's recollections of the events surrounding the group's appearance on the show are not what Harvey Russ, a twenty-five-year-old college student from Georgia, remembered of the experience. He recalled that while waiting backstage prior to being introduced by Springer, the show's producers had brought in a number of Springer show tapes that were subsequently played for the group in the show's Green Room. Since the programs were "only the fighting shows, all the crazy shows," in retrospect Russ believed it was an attempt by the producers "to psych us up." And Cassie Lester, the nineteen-year-old woman "ambushed" by the show as a would-be seducer of gay men, recalled being told "to fight with (her accuser, who appeared incognito), get physical, rip off his disguise. And if me and him don't get physical, get physical with an audience member."

The woman in the California guest group had a remarkably similar recollection. "They kept on getting angry at me because I wasn't getting angry enough on stage," she later recalled. "They said, 'You need to get more angry (sic). You need to stand up and yell. You need to tell them what for . . .' "

According to producer You, however, the opposite is true. "People are always encouraged not to fight and not to swear," she initially said. Only minutes later, though, You confessed the show had been disappointing for just those reasons of supposed encouragement. "Unfortunately, nothing happened on the show," You explained. "On the phone, they were really mad," she confided, "but it wasn't a very good show. There wasn't a real issue."

On a lesser note the Georgia contingent also complained that the show had put them up in below par hotel rooms and had failed to provide certain special perks that had been requested and granted, such as one of the women's husband's stated a desire for White Castle hamburgers. The guests' accusations that the producers and staff gave them the cold shoulder as soon as the taping was over can no doubt be explained by producer You's undisguised disappointment at the group's lack of violent antics during the taping.

Considering that the Springer show tapes 200 shows a year, the disgruntlement among former guests appears to be low. For the most part the guests, with their newly acquired status of TV star, happily enjoy the adulation of their friends, family, and neighbors. For these people, appearing on television has been a healthy and satisfying emotional experience—a much-needed validation of their otherwise routine existence.

"Americans have always had a split personality—we

are Puritans, but we like to break taboos," explains psychologist Ava L. Siegler, author of *The Essential Guide to the New American Adolescence.* "We are becoming a more open culture. Maybe that causes problems. But on the other hand, openness may help create a generation of people who aren't afraid to talk openly about stuff that might embarrass us."

Dr. Richard Campbell, director of the journalism department at Middle Tennessee State University, agrees that an open society is in the making. However, he questions whether *The Jerry Springer Show* is a positive reflection of that openness. "It's a high intensity show that, I think, exploits the private lives of people in a public arena," he explains. "You get a lot of people on the show who should be in some kind of counseling and are using television to air problems. They're putting on a spectacle."

Campbell also believes that the Springer show's success, and that of others of the genre, can be traced directly to an increasing sense of inadequacy and lack of control over their lives by middle- and lower-class Americans. "I think people today feel powerless—like nobody's listening. Bureaucracy has gotten big. Government has gotten big," he says, explaining, "these shows are about people trying to figure out how to get empowered again. I think shows like Jerry Springer pander to that. 'Come on to our show and we'll give you a stage for half an hour and you can do whatever you want—as long as you're in conflict, either verbal or physical.' But," Campbell concludes, "as with any kind of show of this type, this will burn itself out. It's not going to have the staying power of a Donahue or Oprah. Eventually, it'll drop into the sea."

As for the viewers, well, that's an entirely different story. For the observers, whether at home or in the studio audience, the Springer show provides a daily opportunity to indulge in easy morality coupled with the power of pure voyeurism and the normally forbidden delight of sharing a stranger's intimate secrets. The show offers a chance to be politically incorrect in the ethically fixated 1990s, the opportunity to take pleasure in someone else's problems without feeling guilty. It is a pleasure that crosses all lines of endeavor, all ages, all classes, all races. That becomes obvious from even the tiniest glimpse of the Springer show audience—comprised of an amazingly diverse group of people ranging in age from eighteen to octogenarians, all of them enthusiastic in their response to the "human cockfighting" reflected on the program.

"It's white trailer trash! I love it!" exclaimed Paul Unger, a farmer who'd flown from Oregon to Chicago to be a part of Springer's audience. "I hope they fight. They *better* fight," said an eighty-one-year-old grandmother who'd driven in from nearby Indiana with her granddaughter to see a taping of the Springer spectacle.

Alan Brown, a twenty-six-year-old Alabama man, traveled to Chicago to watch the production because he "respects Jerry and his 'Final Thought.' But," he quickly added, "I *really* like the fights."

Linda Nesbit, a fifty-two-year-old Los Angeles woman, likes the show so much that she tapes it every day. "I have fallen out of bed, I laugh so hard. I'll call up my son to get him to turn his set on, and he'll already be looking at it. He'll say, 'Mom, let's get ready to rumble!' "

"Pop culture has become a plop culture—a celebration of all things gloopy, smelly and stomach-churning," penned J. D. Heiman in a recent *New York Post* article. "The craze for crass is even enough to shock residents of New York; the city that nurtured S & M performance art, *Screw* magazine and the subway poster career of a zit doctor."

And, most psychologists and media observers agree, a program such as *The Jerry Springer Show* could only exist in such an era of "plop culture" in which grunge is translated into fashion, pierced and tattooed body parts are considered fashion "statements," loud noise passes for music, and inarticulate cursing masquerades as discourse and communication.

Jerry Springer is absolutely correct when he calls the show "silly, a circus, funny and crazy," a daily outing not to be taken seriously. The problem is that, although Springer repeatedly insists there's nothing fake about the program, the eye gougings, the punches, the hair pulling *are* real—and they're done by supposedly real people. So what's the joke? And who's the butt of it? The very guests he so staunchly defends as having the right to be on his stage, on television. Thus, what it appears he's *really* saying is, "This is America and everyone, rich or poor, educated or uneducated, powerful or powerless, has every right to make a fool of himself or herself if they don't have any better judgment than to appear on my show."

Of course, not everyone who appears on the talk shows and willingly trots out their deepest, darkest secrets—oftentimes along with those of their family and friends and much to the surprise and dismay of all—is simply out on a lark. As hard as they try, the Springer show has had its share of hoaxers—guests who have successfully wound up doing the same thing to those who would have done it to them: made fools out of the show's producers.

CHAPTER NINETEEN

The Canadian Caper

"Dear Jerry Springer," read the e-mail message dated March 4, 1998. "You have frauds on your show. Whether or not you know this, I don't know. You had three people on your show, one transvestite, a guy named Pierce, and a girl. Pierce is not involved with either of them. Pierce is an internet stripper, a porn star trying to be famous. I assure you that this story is completely fabricated. He is from my town, in Toronto, I don't know if you condone stories that are fake; but I thought I would let you know. See ya, Jerry. Al

In early January, 1998, Jerry did an on-line interview with fans from all over the world on Universal Studio's The Backlot Café chat show. One of the most frequently asked questions was how the show's guests were screened to ensure they were genuine. "Well," he'd responded, "that's the job of the producers. The way people come on our show is to call up to tell us their story. As long as the story is outrageous but truthful, they get to be on. The producers make sure they can get whatever evidence they can to verify their story. That can be witnesses, doctor's records, court records. We do our best. Sometimes I've started the show and I know they (the guests) aren't telling the truth. So I've stopped the show.

"Have we ever been fooled? Sure," he admitted. "You don't know the person you're interviewing is always telling the truth. Do we set things up? No. If they come on the show and we find they are not telling the truth, we'll sue them. They have to sign a release to be on that says they are telling the truth and all that stuff. So if you had a gun to my head and asked, 'Does everyone on your show always tell the truth?' I wouldn't say yes. I'm sure some people aren't. We have to do the best we can."

In January, 1995, a quartet of Canadians slipped through the Springer screening process and—masquerading as a husband and wife, babysitter, and boyfriend—turned in a highly dramatic, virtually unforgettable appearance on the show, which was aired the following month. The four were actually members of a Toronto comedy group who had represented themselves as real-life guests with several domestic problems to the Springer show producers. Johnny Gardhouse had portrayed a husband who had had an affair with his children's babysitter, played by Mini Holmes; Suzanne Muir had played the unsuspecting wife; Ian Sirota had played the babysitter's boyfriend.

When the "husband's" affair was revealed to the "wife," the show hit an all-time moment of high drama, with the "wife" screaming accusations and sobbing big tears, then running from the stage. However, after the program had aired on February 7, 1995, the actors were recognized by a number of the show's Canadian viewers, and the story of the hoax immediately hit the news wires. It was only then that the participants admitted they were actually members of a Canadian comedy troupe called The Blockheads.

The Springer show executives were not amused, and subsequently sued the Canadians for production costs and damages, a tidy sum of around $50,000. Now the Canadians are not amused. Nor are they remorseful for having pulled the proverbial wool over the show's producers, two of whom are no longer employed by the show.

The troupe members feel little remorse, partly because they believe the show played dirty with them. For instance, they claim the producers told the "wife" she was going on the show to mend a relationship and told the "husband" it would be better to confess on national television rather than in private.

"In a small, subtle way, they try to incite you to violence," explained Ian Sirota, who played the babysitter's boyfriend. Suzanne Muir, the actress who portrayed "the wife," has been extremely vocal in her feelings about the show as well, claiming the producers essentially lured her from Toronto under false pretenses. "They told me the show was going to be about how to work through problems and put romance back in your marriage," she says. Johnny Gardhouse, who portrayed the errant "husband," also felt the producers were operating on a less than honest premise when they repeatedly told him an on-air confession would be in the best interests of the couple's marriage.

"I said I was worried it would devastate her," Gardhouse claims, adding the producers disagreed. "They told me no, it could turn out a lot worse if I told her off the air," he recalled. "They told me that it really would be a lot better and a lot safer for me to do it on TV. But," he added, "they knew it might turn out very ugly because they asked me if I wanted them to book separate flights for us back to Toronto."

According to Gardhouse and Muir, they were approached after the taping by the now former Springer show producers who offered to pay for two marriage counseling sessions for the distraught "couple" upon their return to Toronto. And, apparently believing the sessions would make a great second outing on the show, the producers had also inquired as to whether or not the twosome would allow them to send a crew to Toronto to videotape them undergoing the therapy!

The Springer show, of course, denied all of these

charges and issued a statement declaring, "We've always been honest and we will continue to be."

In an attempt to ascertain whether the potential guests are for real, the Springer show staff interviews them extensively and does some informal checking into their background, like asking for family photographs, driver's licenses, leases and bills bearing the person's name. As a result, the producers believe that somewhere between 75 and 95% of the people appearing on the show are real people with real problems. So it was a great surprise to everyone, especially Jerry, that these people were frauds, first-class phonies.

"They were good," Springer admits. "They had me going. But this lawsuit is not that we can't take a joke. The only reason these shows have any value in terms of people enjoying them is that you can sit home, scratch your head, and say, 'I can't believe these people are real.' But if they're not real, then you have no show. I know this sounds hypocritical, but you have to protect the reality of your show. You can't let people make up stories on talk shows. You have to set some standards."

Interestingly, the most irate of the show's staff was Richard Dominick, the man responsible for the show's continued descent into the pits of weird and absurd human behavior. Shortly after the program's legal department had filed suit against The Blockheads, an angry Dominick issued his own statement:

> "We feel especially badly (sic) for the people in our audience who felt genuine sympathy for the situation described by these self-proclaimed comics," Dominick thundered in a news release concerning the hoax. "We will not allow our audience to be duped by anyone. We have too much respect for them and for ourselves as journalists."

"We are honest and forthright," added Burt Dubrow, a vice president of Springer's production company. "When people have the audacity to play with our credibility, our fighting gloves come out strong."

"All I have to sell is my honesty," added Springer.

In late April, 1998, Springer's honesty was put to the test when more than a dozen former guests on his show appeared on the syndicated TV magazine *EXTRA* and confessed they had all been coached on what to say, and who to punch, during their appearances. "We acted everything," confessed one of the guests. "They (the producers) wanted us to wrestle and throw each other around. They said, 'We want four fights.'"

Despite the brewing scandal, Springer appeared unfazed by the accusations. In New York City to present an autographed copy of his "Too Hot for TV" video to Planet Hollywood's television archives when the story broke, Springer insisted the stories and the guests on his show are for real. But, he added, if a producer had not followed the show's guidelines "something should be done."

It will be interesting to see if the show's legal "fighting gloves come out strong" against this latest batch of guests as they did against the Canadian comedy troupe because, this time, the credibility of *The Jerry Springer Show* truly *is* in jeopardy. It is the scandal that is not going to go away.

"Of course honesty must have its limits," Eric Zorn, a reporter for the *Chicago Tribune,* responded with more than a hint of sarcasm, "or else how would you ever perform the lofty journalistic function of surprising people with really terrible news, then prodding them with disturbing details. . . ."

Three years later the lawsuit is still pending. And Springer is still trying to sell his vision of honesty, integrity, and journalism to the media. It's been—and remains—pretty much of a lost cause. Unless one considers tabloids such as *The National Enquirer* to be true journalistic efforts, and no one working in the mainstream media does, there is not—and never has been—the remotest link between the antics displayed on *The Jerry Springer Show* and real journalism. Nevertheless, Springer appears undaunted in his quest to tie the two together.

"The only way you get to be on the show is because you want to be on," he explained to an inquiring mind earlier this year. "And you have to sign legal documents stating you want to be on the show, which is another way we are separate from news. On news they will talk about people without regard to the consequences. They can run a story about a personal life, which can ruin a life, marriage, and embarrass children. And yet news runs the story, anyway. They run it because they can get good ratings for it—but it's (often) against people's wishes.

"On our show," he concluded, "we don't talk about anybody unless they want to be on the show. We are probably the *only* talk show on television who *didn't* discuss the O.J. Simpson case."

As for the oft-asked question about whether or not the people appearing as guests on his show are paid for their efforts, Springer's response is adamant. "Never," he responds, "We didn't pay from day one. The truth is," he adds, "although some shows did and still do, we didn't pay from day one because we couldn't afford to pay. Then we didn't pay because we thought people would make up stories for money. Now there's no need. We get thousands of calls a day."

One of the calls the show received was from Dawn Marie Eaves, a twenty-four-year-old Geneva, N.Y., woman who wanted to discuss her love triangle—a twisted affair in which she was having a relationship with the younger brother of the man who had fathered one of her three children. The producers checked out Eaves's story, and when it was verified the woman was invited to come on the show with her current lover as well as her previous lover, his older brother.

The November, 1997, show went along smashingly well, with the audience appropriately gasping—and booing—at Eaves's various romantic revelations, especially the one in which it was learned that the younger brother was only sixteen years old. This particular bit of information, of course, was followed by a slugfest between the two brothers and then a free-for-all between various other guests. In fact, by the time the show had ended, it had become a thoroughly unforgettable Springer outing for its unabashed violence. It had also come to the attention of the Geneva police who promptly arrested Eaves upon her return home, on charges of third degree rape, a felony that carries a maximum four year prison sentence, and endangering the welfare of a child. The judge also issued a protective order barring Eaves from having any contact with the victim. The county also took temporary custody of the woman's children, age two to five years.

"God only knows what effect her conduct has had in respect to these children when she's running around with a sixteen-year-old who happens to be an uncle of one of her young children," declared the prosecutor during Eaves's subsequent court hearing.

For the host and staff of *The Jerry Springer Show*, however, the case of Dawn Marie Eaves was just another magic moment in the annals of the television history they have been building. As Springer confided not long ago, "I'm not sure the topics really matter. It's the same old outrageous relationship kind of topics. We can run the same topic every day and it won't make that much difference.

"What makes it work is the personality of the guests,

how they respond to whatever the situation is in their life at the moment," he had explained. "That's what makes the show go. We don't have any discussion of serious issues on the show. Our show is basically silly, so it's more the personality of the guests than what the subject matter is. I assume it's going to be all love triangles."

Not long after that Springer was asked where he believed so many of these dysfunctional victims that appear as guests on his show came from. He hesitated only momentarily before answering. "They come from us," he replied. "We are the talk show guests of America."

CHAPTER TWENTY

The Carol Marin Fiasco

"Just say Jerry Springer's name, and it is a statement of the kind of television that descends to the lowest rung."

Carol Marin, Reporter

As anyone familiar with the show would suspect, it ultimately would not be only people peripherally involved with *The Jerry Springer Show,* such as The Blockheads, Denny Welch, or Dawn Marie Eaves, who would suddenly find themselves in a whirlwind of controversy. In Spring, 1997, Jerry also found himself in the midst of a left field maelstrom, this one actually not of his own making.

It all began when the management of a Chicago television station, WMAQ, asked Jerry if he would like to be a guest commentator on the station's nightly newscasts during the May ratings sweeps period. Recalling the enjoyment he'd derived from delivering his commentaries on the Cincinnati station, Jerry accepted the offer on a limited basis. He had no idea, nor did station management, as to the furor this new part-time position would create when it was announced he would be delivering "Another Point of View" commentaries on WMAQ, beginning Monday, May 5.

The station's nightly news had been co-anchored for twelve successful years by the team of Carol Marin and Ron Magers, who were dismayed to learn that Jerry was joining their news team. A member of the Chicago Journalism Hall of Fame, Marin did not go quietly along with the plan. Instead, only four days prior to Jerry's long-awaited WMAQ appearance, she delivered her resignation during the nightly newscast. "This isn't about one television newscast in one city," she told viewers. "It's about the heart and soul of news." She then disappeared, but not for long. Only a day later Marin reemerged as a guest on NBC's late night talk show hosted by Tom Snyder. During the show Marin lashed out at WMAQ for having defiled the station's news department by hiring Springer, whom she dubbed "a poster child for the worst television has to offer."

But Marin didn't end her war of words following her sudden angry departure from WMAQ. She continued to badmouth Springer to the local media, telling one interviewer, "Just say Jerry Springer's name, and it is a statement of the kind of television that descends to the lower rung." In a subsequent "guest commentary" in the *Chicago Sun-Times*, she went even further. "Many of us in the trenches of this battle believe that television news is already overwhelmed with too many transient fires, random acts of mayhem, and network programming plugs," she wrote. "And now we see Springer, the poster child for the worst television has to offer, being added to the 10 P.M. news menu."

A media brouhaha of gargantuan proportions immediately erupted into a national story, with the protagonists each appearing on virtually every important national television show to air their thoughts—from *The Tonight Show, Today,* and *ABC World News Tonight* to CNN's *Crossfire* and *The Howard Stern Show.* So great was the ground swell of antagonism that the story made its way into the austere *New York Times,* as well as the *Los Angeles Times, The Washington Post,* and *USA Today,* to name only a few of the nation's major newspapers that carried the story.

Even *TIME* magazine covered the controversy, noting that "Astronauts aren't the only ones who can have a bumpy ride on re-entry," a reference to Springer having once appeared as a news anchorman prior to "wading into the quagmire of daily talk shows." Terming Jerry "the unabashed chronicler of America's most tawdry domestic dramas," the magazine then quipped that asking Marin and Magers to share a show with Springer was similar to beseeching the twosome "to drink battery acid."

And this was *before* Springer's unveiling as the WMAQ commentator. At first Jerry was unperturbed. "What the hell?" he told the *Sun-Times*. "It's only reading a prompter. I mean, they make it seem like it's journalism." To a *Chicago Tribune* reporter he said, "I'm lucky enough to have a national show. Why in the world am I gonna give it up to do local car accidents? If anything, everybody's gotta lighten up. It's local news. It's people talking about what the weather's gonna be tomorrow and what the traffic's like and who got shot the night before." And, he told *TIME*, "No one's grabbing their children off the streets. This is about contract negotiations, not me."

By the end of his first appearance as the WMAQ-TV commentator offering "Another Point of View," however, it had become crystal clear to everyone concerned that the acrimony was not going to subside.

In his first three minute commentary Springer wrapped himself in the American flag, The Holocaust, and the sackcloth of the little guy standing up to the media elite. "Much like his talk show does, he made the issue cheap and ugly," Steve Johnson, a *Chicago Tribune* reporter wrote the following day. "Without naming her, he attacked Marin as a 'Walter Cronkite wannabe' and a practitioner of 'elitist snobbery.' "

Looking straight into the camera, Springer had told the home audience, "I am sorry the anchor quit. I am sorry she found it necessary this week to use me as the stepping-stone to martyrdom." He had then re-

called his status as a former Cincinnati mayor and as
a Jew who had lost his entire family in The Holocaust.
Springer had then segued from that to recalling the
time his father had talked him into allowing a group
of neo-Nazis to march in Cincinnati during his reign
as mayor there because "this is America . . . this is the
freedom we sought when we escaped to here."

Springer had concluded the commentary with a sanc-
timonious "I wish she (Marin) could have met my dad."

It turned out to be an unfortunate choice of subject
matter. The following day *The Cincinnati Enquirer* took
Springer to task for having exaggerated his role in de-
termining whether or not the neo-Nazi parade would
take place and pointed out it was the safety director,
not the ceremonial mayor, who issued such permits.

In Chicago the backlash against Springer was immediate and brutal. Within minutes of Springer's debut,
the WMAQ "feedback line" that had been installed for
viewer response to his commentaries had become over-
loaded. In the final tally 1,467 Chicagoans had tele-
phoned the station to say they did not support Springer
and would no longer watch the WMAQ news; fifty-six
callers said they did not appreciate his mentioning The
Holocaust or attacking Marin; twenty callers wondered
what management was thinking by hiring Springer; and
six callers declared Carol Marin thought too highly of
herself. Only fifty-seven of the callers had had anything
positive to say about Springer's addition to the newscast
or his initial commentary.

The next day a review of Springer's Monday night
debut was splashed across the front page of the *Chicago
Sun-Times* in a headline that read: "Springer Fights
Back, First Commentary Blasts Marin."

"Springer seems to feel he can separate his daytime
persona from his nightly commentaries," penned Richard Roeper, a *Sun-Times* columnist. "After all, he's not

really like that rabid ringmaster who orchestrates the daily circus of the grotesque on his syndicated show."

The *Chicago Tribune* simply reviewed the appearance, accusing Springer of using "wild and extreme imagery" in his commentary. "As on his daytime talk show," wrote Steve Johnson, "where he exploits people's pain for profit and then pretends to try to help them with advice, he was intellectually dishonest. Here, it was in his characterization of the reason for Marin's stand against him."

The most savage criticism, however, was authored by Jeff Borden, a reporter for *Crain's Chicago Business,* who penned, "On the first night, he lived down to his reputation. I thought it (Springer's commentary) was sad and pathetic. It was a classless, mean-spirited rant."

Even members of the Chicago academia became involved in the media storm. "It was a mistake to have Jerry Springer as a commentator," noted Patricia Dean, chair of the broadcast program at Northwestern University's vaunted Medill School of Journalism. "And when he made a factual error on the air and then brushed it off as if the factual error didn't matter, it was the overall story and impression he was trying to make—that's the difference between entertainment and journalism. In journalism, the facts matter."

Marin was in Los Angeles, preparing for a guest appearance on *The Late Late Show with Tom Snyder* the night Springer delivered his commentary. She issued only a brief statement. "I'm not a martyr. I'm not the Mother Teresa of journalism. I'm a reporter."

On Tuesday evening Jerry delivered his second commentary, this one a homily about churchgoing in America and free choice, which turned out to be his final WMAQ appearance. On Wednesday night the station withheld Springer's commentary and instead offered a news report on the allegations that Springer's first commentary had exaggerated his authority to issue neo-Nazis, or anyone else, for that matter, a parade permit.

Springer's response to the accusation he "fibbed" was interesting. "Obviously the city manager is the one who puts his signature on it," Springer retorted, "but it was a sensitive issue, a hot issue, so the city manager and safety director came to me in my office and said, 'What do you want to do with this?' " Springer claimed to have told them he wanted his parents' response to the issue. If they were offended, he'd supposedly told the two city officials, "You'll have to find someone else for your mayor. That's exactly what happened," he told John Kiesewetter, a *Cincinnati Enquirer* reporter. "I've spoken about it for years."

By Thursday it no longer mattered what had truly transpired almost twenty years before. Jerry wanted no part of "Another Point of View." He sent a note to Lyle Banks, the station's general manager, that afternoon, telling him, "It's gotten too personal . . . Right now it's probably not worth it, considering the flak and all."

WMAQ then issued its own statement. "We respect Jerry's decision to stop his commentaries, and we sincerely regret the personal attacks he has endured. Over the last few days, we have heard from a number of viewers, many of whom disagreed with our decision to put Mr. Springer on the air. We appreciate the feedback and feel we are being responsible to it." Jerry was relieved that it had all come to an end. "This is my happiest day in a week," he told his staff. "Enough is enough."

The turmoil had finally ended. Or had it?

Three weeks after Springer had abandoned "Another Point of View," the controversy took another unexpected and strange twist when a letter from George Clooney, the heartthrob of NBC's hit series *ER*, arrived at the network's Chicago affiliate, and set the town ablaze with chatter once again. Addressed to the station management, and subsequently published by the *Chicago Tribune,* the letter read:

May 27, 1997

"I just wanted to send a quick note to my friends at WMAQ, and congratulate them on the hiring of Jerry Springer. Even if he is gone now.

"I'm proud to be part of a network that finally just admits that news has become pure entertainment.

"Since I happen to be in the entertainment industry and have a little history with local news (my father was an anchorman), and Jerry Springer (I've known him most of my life, and my father gave him his first broadcasting job), I thought I'd give you some pointers.

1. Put a tote board behind the desk numbering off people killed that day. You know . . . break it into categories.
2. Ring a bell off every time a child is abducted or missing.
3. Do a five-part series on string bikinis—good or bad. (Scratch that, you did it for last month's sweeps.)
4. Fire all the other on air people who stand up for journalism (they can cause trouble).
5. Get Siegfried & Roy to do the sports and weather. (Siegfried likes sports.)
6. Get Jerry back to cover other stories. Let him do a sweeps piece on why it's dumb to write checks to hookers in Cincinnati. (Something he's an expert on.)
7. Give free Cadillacs to anyone in the Chicago area who watches your news and learns anything of value or truth (you'll save a lot of money there).
8. And finally, never, never kid yourself that Jerry

Springer is a journalist or that you are anything
more than a tabloid show with nicer hair.

You should be embarrassed.

I applaud the anchors who left.

—George Clooney, TV actor

At first Jerry had been terribly wounded by what he
would later term the "unwarranted" and "vicious" attacks by the press. "All my political fights in life I chose—
or because of my behavior I had to answer for," he told
a reporter, adding, "but I had nothing to do with this.
They asked me to do some commentaries, and I said
'Yes.' And then she went ballistic . . . and I was thrown
into the middle of this. I would love for someone to tell
me what I did that was evil. They asked *me,*" he empha-
sized. "It wasn't my idea. Next time don't ask!"

For a while, Springer would later confess, he even felt
guilty about having been the catalyst for Marin's departure from the station. As time passed, however, he grew
angry. Now he views the entire fiasco as one of life's
many learning lessons.

"I was pretty much the fool, not knowing the whole
story when I took the commentary position," he concedes. "I thought at the time she was quitting because
I was coming on. But the truth was she had already
been informed that WMAQ was not renewing her contract. That she was out. And then when I came on, she
announced that I was the reason. Well, if I had known
at the time I would have said, 'Excuse me, tell me the
truth. You weren't rehired.' But when I talk to people
walking around the streets, they still believe she quit
because I came on. Not true. She wasn't being renewed.
There *was* no principle involved. It was ugly for a week."

Yes, but that "week" *was* the first week of May, which signifies the all-important ratings "sweeps" month in videoland. It is in fact the time period in which TV advertising rates are set for the rest of the year. How fortuitous for the station that such a publicity *blitzkrieg* should occur during that particular duration. Moreover, according to Lyle Banks, the station manager, Marin *had* been informed more than a week before her dramatic on-air resignation that the station "was going in another direction" and, as a result, her contract was not going to be renewed. "I regret the misperception of her departure," he later told a reporter on the very day he received Jerry's resignation letter.

All facts considered, it's no small wonder some industry insiders believe the whole thing was a ratings stunt on the part of WMAQ and a self-serving stance by Carol Marin who, in July, 1997, signed a very lucrative, multi-year contract with the CBS network. The contract allows her to remain in Chicago as the head of a special network news unit yet gives her network exposure as a reporter on Bryant Gumbel's prime time CBS-TV news magazine.

Whatever the truth, the fact is that Jerry Springer did not emerge unscathed from the experience. Nor did he gain anything from it, other than possibly some sleepless nights. And he certainly didn't need to boost his ratings. At that point, his show was already being watched by nearly 6.7 million Americans.

"I'm sure it helped (the show's ratings)," he would later admit, "but I'd rather it not have happened because it was just so dishonest. I feel more upset at that now than I did then. Because then I felt, 'Oh, gosh, did I really cause her to quit?' And since it wasn't my job, I didn't feel really good about it. If it were my full-time job, I wouldn't have cared. I would have said, 'Hey, if you can't handle it, it's just too bad.' "

CHAPTER TWENTY-ONE

Jerry Springer: Pop Icon

"I admit I'm a little old for this connection, but I'm not threatening to young people. I'm their uncle. Their crazy uncle."

Jerry Springer

"Once your show catches on," Springer said not long ago, "it's almost like a geometric progression, because then everyone starts talking about it around the water cooler at work, and before you realize it you've doubled your audience as those people start watching. Now it's like a runaway train. We're going through the roof, and I'm just trying to hold on." There are those, however, who are beginning to believe, half in jest at least, that Jerry might be *losing* his grip instead.

For example, by February, 1998, Springer had begun telling interviewers that double standards operated viewing habits, meaning anyone who didn't like his show apparently was a hypocrite, and that the biggest hypocrites of all were not talk shows but TV media.

"I was probably more hypocritical doing the news than doing the talk show," he confessed to a *Dallas Morning News* writer. "I would do the news with a serious face. But we were in the same business, trying to get ratings. We exploited people by constantly jamming a microphone into their faces, whether they wanted to be on TV or not. We didn't have any regard for how it affected their lives or their families. At least with a talk show, no one gets on except those who really, really, really want to get on."

He'd also begun speaking strangely, as though *The Jerry Springer Show* had a depth, a substance, perhaps even a purpose to which only *he,* the host, was privy. This first became noticeable when Jerry began comparing *his* show to the heartfelt revelations of her ruined marriage and subsequent eating disorder by the late Princess of Wales during *her* television interview. Conducted from within the hallowed, calm walls of Kensington Palace, the Diana interview was a study in graciousness and proper English. No one in their right mind would consider comparing *that* program to a show bearing the name Jerry Springer and emanating from the anything but calm fake brick confines of a Chicago studio, unless, of course, that person *was* Jerry Springer.

"Remember Princess Diana was on TV saying she was unfaithful and had bulemia and was contemplating suicide?" Jerry asked a reporter. "Yeah. When famous people talk about these intimate and personal issues it is considered perfectly acceptable. But if it's people who are not rich or famous or powerful, people say we cannot have that on TV. The success of my show demonstrates that people want to know about them, too."

Wrong. The Diana interview offered a meaningful, provocative view of royal reality. By Jerry's own admission, his show is "meant to be made fun of. It's chewing gum. It's an hour of escape. If you've had a tough day and want to escape for a bit, this will do it for you." So how do you justify the thought that viewers want "to learn" about the guests on the Springer show? You don't, no matter how hard you try or how much rhetoric you speak. Viewers tune in and people show up for the tapings because they want to see real people *fighting,* not talking, which—considering the cursing, the bleeps and the inability of most of them to convey even the most simplistic of thoughts—is probably a mercy. Princess Di, on the other hand, was a talker, an international role model, who had the good sense to save *her* temper tantrums for the privacy of her palace. When she spoke in public it was in clear, articulate simple sentences. Find that on any of the Jerry Springer shows.

But Jerry didn't stop with the Princess Di defense. A few weeks later he had the temerity to compare his show with *M*A*S*H*, the classic comedy series starring Alan Alda, telling a reporter, "I've done the show for seven years, and just signed for five more. So twelve years for a show, that's a pretty good run. *M*A*S*H* was only on for eleven years, so I have nothing to complain about. I'm very grateful."

The comparison of *his* show with *M*A*S*H* was interesting, perhaps even telling, because that series is recognized as one of the all-time *finest* shows in the history of television. *The Jerry Springer Show,* on the other hand, will forever be remembered as one of the medium's absolute *worst,* daytime or nighttime. But, hey, this is America, a land—at least in Jerry's mind—where everyone's entitled to his minute of fame, or shame, in front of the microphone, no matter how big a fool he or she makes of himself or herself, no matter how rich he or she makes Jerry Springer at his or her own expense.

And rich he is fast becoming.

He has just signed a multi-million dollar contract to host the show for five more years, which will take the Springer show into the new millenium, providing both the show and host last that long. And he owes it all to having become virtually overnight an MTV pop culture icon.

As Richard Dominick predicted two years ago when he sold Springer on turning the show into a Roman coliseum of sorts, Jerry has captured the hearts, perhaps even the minds, of the David Letterman crowd. "That changed everything," Springer now admits. "That freed me to be an entertainer, that and leaving television news.

I constantly had this conflict because I couldn't have the same persona doing the show as I had doing the news."

Whatever the reasons behind his success, the fact is that Jerry has become the idol of the nation's Generation Xers and college students, all of whom regard the show as an entertaining spectacle and view him as a unique combination of ringmaster, father figure, and, if you can believe it, sex symbol. As a result, *The Jerry Springer Show* is now the top-rated nationally syndicated program for men and women ages eighteen to twenty-four. It's an amazing transformation for a fifty-four-year-old bespectacled self-confessed *schlub* from Queens via the Midwest, hardly sex symbol turf, which may explain why it is a mantle of rosy-cheeked adulation Springer does not appear to wear comfortably.

"I think it's that I'm so uncool that it's come full circle," he recently joked, adding, "maybe they feel sorry for me." And, to an interviewer, he confided, "I admit I'm a little old for this connection, but I'm not threatening to young people. I'm their uncle. Their *crazy* uncle." Richard Dominick concurs. "Jerry's a real nice guy. He's like the uncle you can't wait to have come over," he confided to a reporter recently. "He has a calming influence." Well, maybe Jerry has a calming influence on the show, not a particularly difficult chore given the highly-charged behavior of the guests. But it was anything but calm when "Uncle" Jerry dropped by the University of Tampa several months ago. Springer was given a hero's welcome by 800 cheering students who'd packed the school's Falk Theatre to participate in a typical Springer question and answer session. "He's almost like a father figure to the kids," explained Grant Donaldson, the school's public affairs director.

Thus, whether traveling as a crazy uncle or father figure, Jerry has become a most sought after guest on the lucrative college campus circuit, even flying to merry

Olde England in March to deliver a lecture on freedom of speech, his favorite subject, at Oxford University. While he was there he picked up some extra bucks in London speaking before an audience of 1,000 people attending a fundraiser organized by the London L'Chaim Society. That same month he appeared in Philadelphia to stage a mock version of *The Jerry Springer Show* for students at Temple University.

It seems the only place Jerry Springer *won't* be found this year is at the Emmy Awards ceremony. In the seven years his show has been on the air it has yet to receive a nomination. He also won't be writing his autobiography any time soon. The William Morris Agency has tried to talk him into penning his memoirs for five years. So far he's declined, telling them, "I don't know what to write about. I don't want to do an autobiography. That's a fluff book. I won't do that. If I wrote a book I would write a political book, and I need more time than I've got right now for that. That's the problem. And I won't do an as told to with someone. If I'm writing a book, *I'm* writing the book."

All that glistens is not necessarily talk for Springer, either. He's become a commodity on the acting circuit, as well. Last December he appeared on the popular Fox Television series, *The X-Files,* portraying himself, of course. It was a black and white episode based on the unusual combination of the Frankenstein legend, the movie *Mask,* and other recycled pop culture, all of which had been spun into a far out yarn by Chris Carter, the show's creator and a Springer show fan. Prior to that Jerry had appeared on the Fox Network in an episode of *Married . . . with Children* as a punch line for Al Bundy.

More recently, Jerry appeared in cameo roles, again playing himself, in two films—*Kissing a Fool,* a romantic comedy set in Chicago and starring David Schwimmer and Bonnie Hunt, and *Meet Wally Sparks*, a comedy starring Rodney Dangerfield as the host of a tabloid TV show. Considering the parallels between the *reel* and the *real* TV show, it's not surprising that the movie's producers chose to include Springer.

In the film, for instance, Wally Sparks is under attack from family value groups and his sponsors are pulling their commercials. Why? Because of the program's deranged segments, such as when a man who has left his wife for the family dog appears as a guest, only to be confronted by his irate wife. "That bitch!" she hisses. Unfortunately, unlike the Springer show, the movie was short-lived at the box office and quickly wound up on video shelves, where it also did meager business.

Perhaps Springer's most unforgettable appearance, outside of his own show, of course, was his February, 1998, guest spot on *MAD TV,* in which he did a devastating parody of himself and his show.

Later asked *why,* Jerry had replied: "Well, because it's worth parodying. I mean, it's the most foolish show in the world and, you know it's great fun to do. I mean, that's the whole point of the show, to make fun of it. I'd hate to do a show that I couldn't make fun of. It's obviously a silly, stupid show and it's meant to be that. It's a cultural cartoon. It's not meant to be serious. It's comedy, most of the time. I mean, once in a while it's serious, but generally it's just comedy."

Parody and cultural cartoon aside, Jerry's appearance on the show not only paid him, it paid off in publicity as well. To draw attention to Springer being on the show, the *MAD* producers sent out a press release accompanied by an Alfred E. Newman snow globe and a greeting card to the nation's TV critics. The text of the release read:

> *"Please accept this gift on behalf of* MAD TV. *We think you are one of the finest critics in the business, and know that you would never compromise your integrity by giving our show a rave review just because we bought you a little something.*
>
> *"That's why we shelved the idea of sending you a stripper and a case of booze. (Besides, that would have cost us a fortune and these snowball thingies fell off the back of a truck in front of our studio.) So why not take another look at our show. Say February 28? Jerry Springer's gonna host and we've got a great idea for a sketch where the studio audience beats the crap out of HIM! We haven't told him yet, so please don't mention it in your review."*

In early Spring Jerry managed to find time to sit down long enough to be interviewed by *Playboy* magazine, to travel to Negril, Jamaica, to host two MTV "Springer Break" specials, both of which were as sophomoric as his daily show, and to participate in an hour long *E! Entertainment* documentary called *E! The True Story.* He also appeared in taped segments on *Access Hollywood* and *Entertainment Tonight.* Then, accompanied by his chief of security Steve Wilkos, and his stage manager, Todd Schiltz, he flew to Hollywood to tape a guest appearance on the comedy series, *Between Brothers,* the top-rated show among black viewers. That the *Brothers* producers invited Jerry to appear as a guest is testament to an ironic fact: according to a study by TN Media, Jerry Springer is the black community's favorite talk show host, while Oprah Winfrey is the favorite among white viewers.

Leaving no public relations stone unturned, in April Jerry even popped up on the hipper than hip *RuPaul Show* on cable's VH1 Network where, appearing weary and wary, he obliquely answered the drag queen's questions, including whether or not he/she could get on his show. "You're not crazy enough to get on our show," Springer replied.

Later, in response to the oft-asked question, "Are those people on your show for real?" he good-naturedly confessed, "The guests are real. I'm fake!"

In late April Jerry even turned up on the syndicated Fox television series, *America's Most Wanted*, to help the FBI track down fugitive Jeffrey Durham, who had appeared on his show in 1996 in an episode titled "Men Living as Women." Durham had gone on the show as the boyfriend of a preoperative transsexual named "Amber" whom, he told Springer, he had met in a laundromat. Not true. The pair had actually met in prison.

"The truth is that this guy is a major bad guy," said a spokesman for *America's Most Wanted*. "He has a horrible temper, semiautomatic weapons and he breaks into people's homes."

Despite his busy schedule, it should be noted that Springer still finds the energy to devote some of his time to a number of worthwhile causes. He has co-hosted *The Jerry Lewis Muscular Dystrophy Labor Day Telethon* for the past three years, and last year was elected to serve as Vice-President of the National Muscular Dystrophy Association. He also serves on the advisory board of the Audrey Hepburn Hollywood for Children Fund, an umbrella foundation formed to continue the late actress's work for needy children around the world for several years. On his own, Jerry also established a scholarship fund several years ago at the Kellman School in Chicago, an institution dedicated to improving the standard of education for inner city youth.

These days, however, he has little time to devote to anything other than his career. Springer fever is most definitely in the air. *Dateline. Nightline. Primetime Live. 20/20. Chicago Hope.* Producers. Directors. Celebrities. Reporters. Publishers. Everybody, it seems, wants Jerry

Springer. They want him on their show, on their pages, on their hats or T-shirts, at their fundraisers, on their stage or, as in the case of his detractors, they want him off the air. And if they're not talking *with* him, they're talking *about* him—and not just on the news. This season he's had his name mentioned on *ER, Law & Order, The Tonight Show, The David Letterman Show* and *Ellen,* to name only a few. Nor does the pace appear to be slowing.

Springer recently signed a $2 million movie deal with producer Steve Stabler, whose past projects include the comedy films, *Dumb and Dumber* and *Kingpin,* for a film based on his talk show; and there have also been rumors of a sitcom series.

Jerry, of course, is taking it all in his typical low-keyed, good-natured stride. "Everything comes at once," he says. "All those years you struggle, you think, 'Where is everybody?' Now I want to play everything. You don't get two shots at this. I want to experience as much as I can before the energy goes—or the hair goes."

Springer is more than aware that the attention now being showered on him and his show will not last forever. There will come a time, perhaps soon, when the audience will tire of watching those hair-pulling hussies and angry mothers-in-law pushing and shoving each other. After all, viewers tired of watching televised wrestling, which, in truth, is not all that far removed from the antics displayed on *The Jerry Springer Show.*

And then what?

"Then we change." He laughed. "If the public no longer wants what we're giving them, we change. That's the beauty of this show. The only thing that's permanent are the chairs."

As it turns out, even the chairs may not be permanent. On the day the scandal involving sixteen former guests, all of whom charged their appearances were scripted and the fight scenes were choreographed, hit the airwaves the Springer show was canceled by WMAQ-TV, the station who had once briefly hired Springer as a commentator on its evening news. Less than 24 hours later, however, it was announced that WFLD, a Fox-owned station in Chicago, would begin carrying the Springer show.

Ironically, the news of the show's cancellation by WMAQ arrived only the day before a "Dump Jerry Springer!" coalition of Chicagoland religious leaders and activists were scheduled to march in front of the NBC Tower, which houses both the station and the Springer show, to protest WMAQ's telecast of the show.

Upon learning of the switch in stations, the protestors quickly changed directions and marched on WFLD instead!

"We're here to say: wake up and smell the trash," explained Father Michael Pfleger, leader of the coalition. "We're holding everyone who supports *The Jerry Springer Show* accountable until it is off the air."

After his contract ends he says he'll probably get out of the spotlight, perhaps become a political science professor, or maybe a used car salesman. "To be honest," he confided, "who knows? I never map anything out. I've been everything you can't respect in life. I've been a lawyer, a mayor, a news anchor and a talk show host. Once I become a used car salesman I'll have done the whole cycle."

CHAPTER TWENTY-TWO

Dr. Talk

"Up on the stage, some gals who look like leftovers from the Hee-Haw show gather around a side bank of microphones. Springer loops a guitar around his neck; he also holds a crib sheet to the lyrics in one hand—which might explain the presence of the heavy fogging machines that have started polluting the air.

"At the break between takes, Springer grabs the standing microphone and pulls it towards him, while swiveling his hips. He starts singing a sexy ballad, his delivery part Elvis, part The Big Bopper. Then he breaks himself up. It's all just a goof for him."

In 1995 Jerry added yet another dimension to his resumé by becoming a country singer/songwriter. That was the year he penned "Dr. Talk," which he then recorded as the title song of a CD bearing the same name. He later recorded a music video of the song in Bub City, a Chicago barbecue restaurant decorated to look like a Texas roadhouse. The video and the CD were released the following summer. Unlike his TV talk show, however, they did not reach any heights and are now improbably collector's items, even though Jerry again put his best efforts into plugging his music.

Although he had been interested in music and had played the guitar since he was a youngster, according to Jerry his interest in country music wasn't aroused the summer he took Katie to a Billy Ray Cyrus show at the Grand Ole Opry in Nashville. "As I was listening to all the music it dawned on me that the subject matter is the same as talk shows—divorce, broken relationships, pickup trucks, cheatin', who slept with whose dog," he recalled not long ago. "Basically country is a talk show put to music. So I tried writing a song, one thing led to another, and then I recorded it. But you can't sell the CD with just one song, so I had to record eight covers to go along with my original."

Jerry then went on tour with Billy Ray Cyrus, appearing as the opening act during several stops on Billy Ray's Redneck Heaven tour. "What I am most worried about is remembering the words without cue cards," he explained just prior to appearing at one of the concerts. "On the show I just talk. If I could get on stage and make up words, I would be fine. But they want you to sing the words of the song. Maybe I'll just make stuff up."

The "Dr. Talk" CD, which features Springer singing old country favorites, a few modern folk-rock tunes, leftovers from his days at Tulane and Northwestern, as well as his original title song, was released on the Fiddlefish Music label and quickly disappeared. Not only wasn't the public interested in listening to Jerry sing, the nation's music reviewers were outspokenly unimpressed by Springer's musical endeavors. "Don't Quit Your Day Job," penned a writer in *Electronic Media Magazine* in January, 1996. "Springer's rendition of 'Mr. Tambourine Man' sounds like something you'd hear in a kareoke bar," reported the music critic for the *Akron Beacon*.

As usual, Jerry was fearless. He's never had any illusions about the quality of his singing or guitar playing. He's also never been reticent to get up on stage and perform anywhere, for anyone, at any time. In 1994, for instance, Jerry had been having a drink in the dark confines of Los Angeles' Viper Room—the notorious Sunset Boulevard club owned by Johnny Depp where actor River Phoenix took his last drink and his last breath several years ago—when the urge to perform suddenly came upon him. Jumping up on stage he launched into a medley of Elvis Presley tunes, to the delighted amusement of the band and the audience.

He repeated that performance not long afterward, this time at Chicago's Whiskey River nightclub, again offering audiences his version of Elvis Presley singing "I Want You, I Need You, I Love You" and "Love Me Tender." For the Chicago performance, it was reported, he donned an Elvis cape which, said one onlooker, made him look like a cross between Elvis and the late Roy Orbison, since beneath the cape he was wearing black jeans and a black leather jacket. "I will never convince myself I'm any good," Springer confided to a friend not long ago. "My theory," he added, "is that people will tolerate almost anything when they're drinking."

TWENTY-THREE

A Final Thought

Although he's certainly become far richer and more famous than he was during his years as a politician and nightly news commentator back in Cincinnati, the truth is that nothing much has really changed in regard to Jerry Springer. He's still jumping on stage, doing his Elvis Presley imitations. He's still plucking his guitar and singing. He's still delivering nightly commentaries and calling them "A Final Thought." And, although he hasn't wrestled a bear in the last twentysomething years, he did suit up and play goalie for the Milwaukee Admirals hockey team last year.

What's really unchanged, however, is that his detractors are essentially utilizing the same adjectives to assess his character today as they were two decades ago when a political columnist for *The Cincinnati Enquirer* wrote:

"There is a chemistry about Springer that evokes both intense affection and intense dislike. Many see him as a charismatic, idealistic, dynamic, public official, sincerely interested in the causes he espouses. But others regard him as an opportunistic charlatan, a headline grabber who plays to the crowd for his own ego gratification."

Of course, there is one distinctive difference. In those early days, the media was assessing Springer as a politician. Today they're critiquing him as an entertainer, which once again proves there *really* is very little difference between the two endeavors. Or perhaps it's the consistency of the man himself.

Jerry was then, and is now, a man of contradictions able to simultaneously promulgate two distinctly different thoughts. He can one moment claim the only thing the "silly, crazy, outrageous" Springer show rejects is "normal" people, and in the same breath label anyone who suggests the show is sleazy to be "elitist" for not wanting to see these "regular people" on his show. It's an intriguing thought pattern that has obviously served him well as he's traveled the path from politics to news and, ultimately, to sheer *nonsense*.

APPENDIX

How To Talk Yourself On To TV

The Springer show has spawned everything from an amazing variety of talk show web sites, where show devotees discuss their favorite hosts, cut up the performances by guests, and compare notes on who came out on top in the last on-air fight, on the Internet. One of the most intriguing sites, however, is *The Official Talk Show Web Site* created by Trevor Reiger, an enthusiastic groupie of all talk shows. An enterprising young man, Reiger has turned his passion into a cottage industry, filling the site with monthly listings of what's what and who's who on the talk shows, biographies of the various hosts, and a myriad of statistics ranging from the interesting to the inane.

He also uses the web site to promote The National Talk Show Guest Registry, which claims to be "the first clearinghouse in the world for individuals who would like to share their personal life adventures with a TV audience.

"If you're ready to share your true personal stories and real-life experiences with a large audience, The National Talk Show Guest Registry is the place for you!

"Take aim at your 15 MINUTES of fame today!

"If you're booked, you could receive FREE air travel to the show's location, FREE hotel accommodations, FREE ground transportation, up to $50 per day meal-money and even wage reimbursement if you need to take time off from work to be a guest!''

Apparently it's worked for Reiger, whose web site is filled with color photos of—you guessed it—himself posing with every talk show host of the last five years, from Bey to Springer. No doubt his success in the talk show circuit has caused Trevor to also take pen in hand to offer *Secrets, Tips and Tricks on How To Get on Talk Shows,* a ten dollar guide filled with information on talk show behavior.

Jerry Springer Statistics

Birthday: February 13, 1944

Place of Birth: London

Childhood Residence: Moved to Queens, N.Y. when he was five years old

Height and weight: 5 feet, 11 inches; 168 pounds

Education: Tulane University, earned degree in political science, 1965; Northwestern University, law degree, 1968

Family: wife, Micki; daughter, Katie

Religion: Jewish

Hobbies: playing guitar, reading, watching sports

Career: lawyer, politician, TV news anchorman and commentator, talk show host

Awards: Seven Emmys for news commentary

Favorite Transportation: a black stretch limousine

Favorite Sport: Baseball

Favorite Team: The New York Yankees

Favorite Food: Chocolate ice cream

Favorite Movie: *Gone With The Wind*

Favorite Publication: The Nielsen Ratings report

Favorite Quote: His own—"I may not be right, but I'm not far from it."

Favorite Impersonation: His own—of Elvis Presley

Source List

Amarillo Globe News
Associated Press
Broadcasting & Cable Magazine
The Cincinnati Enquirer
Chicago Tribune
Chicago Cigar Smoker Magazine
The Cincinnati Post
The Detroit News
Entertainment Weekly
Fox News on-line
London Jewish Chronicle
Los Angeles Times
MacLean's magazine
The Miami Herald
Newsday
New York Daily News
New York Post
Official Jerry Springer Press Biography
Orange County Register
People
Philadelphia Inquirer
Salon Magazine
Time magazine
This is London
TV Guide
TV Talk Shows website
Universal Studios on-line interview
UPI
U.S. News & World Report

USA Today
Virginia AP
The Washington Post

CELEBRITY BIOGRAPHIES

BARBRA STREISAND   (0-7860-0051-1, $4.99/$5.99)
By Nellie Bly

BURT AND ME   (0-7860-0117-8, $5.99/$6.99)
By Elaine Blake Hall

CAPTAIN QUIRK   (0-7860-0185-2, $4.99/$5.99)
By Dennis William Hauck

ELIZABETH: (0-8217-4269-8, $4.99/$5.99)
   THE LIFE OF ELIZABETH TAYLOR
By Alexander Walker

JIMMY STEWART:
   A WONDERFUL LIFE   (0-7860-0506-8, $5.99/$7.50)
By Frank Sanello

MARLON BRANDO:
   LARGER THAN LIFE   (0-7860-0086-4, $4.99/$5.99)
By Nellie Bly

OPRAH!   (0-8217-4613-8, $4.99/$5.99)
   UP CLOSE AND DOWN HOME
By Nellie Bly

RAINBOW'S END:
   THE JUDY GARLAND SHOW   (0-8217-3708-2, $5.99/$6.99)
By Coyne Steven Sanders

THE KENNEDY MEN: (1-57566-015-6, $22.95/$26.95)
   3 GENERATIONS OF SEX, SCANDAL, & SECRETS
By Nellie Bly

TODAY'S BLACK HOLLYWOOD   (0-7860-0104-6, $4.99/$5.99)
By James Robert Parish

Available wherever paperbacks are sold, or order direct from the Publisher. Send cover price plus 50¢ per copy for mailing and handling to Kensington Publishing Corp., Consumer Orders, or call (toll free) 888-345-BOOK, to place your order using Mastercard or Visa. Residents of New York and Tennessee must include sales tax. DO NOT SEND CASH.